PAST and PRESENT

No 67

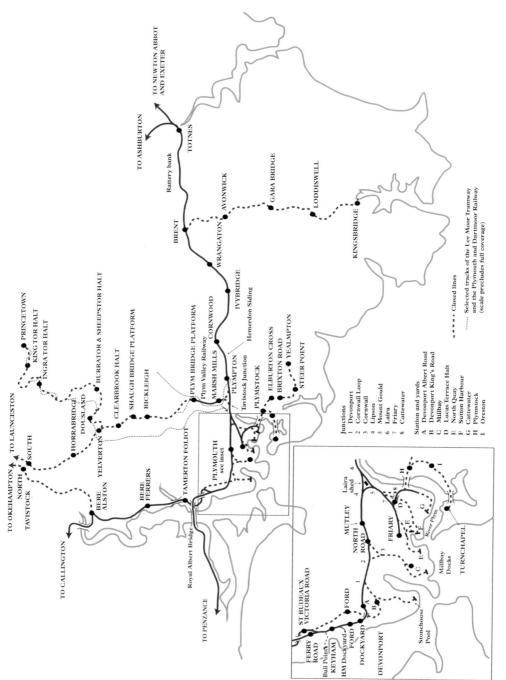

Map of the area covered by this book, showing locations featured or referred to in the text.

BRITISH RAILWAYS

PAST and PRESENT

No 67

Plymouth & South West Devon

David Mitchell

Past & Present Publishing Ltd

First published in 2013

British Library Cataloguing in Publication Data

A catalogue record for this book is available from the British Library.

ISBN 978 1 85895 271 0
Past & Present Publishing Ltd
The Trundle
Ringstead Road
Great Addington
Kettering
Northants NN14 4BW

Tel/Fax: 01536 330588
email: sales@nostalgiacollection.com
Website: www.nostalgiacollection.com

Printed and bound in the Czech Republic

NEAR INGRA TOR HALT: Just a few months from withdrawal, Laira's last '4400' Class 2-6-2T No 4410 is about half a mile east of the halt as it crosses the valley of the Yes Tor Brook with the 12.08pm train from Princetown to Yelverton on Saturday 23 April 1955. These smaller-wheeled 'Prairies' were ideally suited to the branch's stiff gradients and sharp curves, and worked the line for about 50 years. Usually an engine spent a week on the branch before being changed, and was stabled at Princetown overnight. The disused Swelltor Quarries are on the distant hillside.

In the Introduction to the original Devon volume in this series, I commented on how the county's mild climate had contributed to many scenes becoming totally overgrown. In the 22 years since, matters have generally become worse in this respect, and it is now often even more difficult to replicate a 'past' scene – an activity also hindered by a 'growth' in fencing and buildings! It was therefore a particular pleasure to explore the remains of the Princetown branch on a bright early autumn day in 2012. Visiting Dartmoor is of course always a joy, but a paucity of trees and other vegetation on the high moor also meant that it was a far easier proposition to align a facsimile photograph. *Peter F. Bowles, R. Woodley collection/DHM*

CONTENTS

NEAR DEVONPORT JUNCTION: The Great Western and Southern main lines shadowed each other for much of their respective routes through Plymouth; indeed, even after it had established its own route into the city, the latter had to use rights on more than 3 miles of the former's track to reach its terminus. Plymouth was also similar to Exeter, its Devon rival, in that due to their different approaches to the city, Western and Southern trains bound for the same destination would travel in opposite directions from one another. Ex-GWR 'Mogul' No 5339 is heading east as it approaches Devonport Junction in the 1950s. The WR line is at a higher level to the right. The use of WR engines on the SR route (and vice versa) between Plymouth and Exeter was a regular feature for more than 20 years, thus enabling crews from each Region to maintain their knowledge of the other's line. This meant that, in case of emergency, trains could be easily re-routed without the need for pilot men. The train is possibly the 11.47am Exeter Central to Friary, a regular 'exchange duty'.

The cutting was slowly filled in after closure, the work being completed in the early 1980s, and is now Stoke Damerel Park. To the right, the WR route is very overgrown; the 1400 Penzance to Paddington HST approaches on 1 October 2012. *Peter F. Bowles, R. Woodley collection/DHM (2)*

INTRODUCTION

After a hiatus we resume our anti-clockwise tour of Devon's railways, commencing in Tavistock where the previous volume, No 53 *North and West Devon*, ended. One benefit of this delay is that, due to the amount of material collected, there will now be a fourth title covering South Devon. Although this volume features a relatively small area, it is a corner of the county that provides great contrasts, with urban Plymouth figuring prominently, yet with a rural hinterland that in itself also provides much scenic variety.

Plymouth lies between the Rivers Plym and Tamar and commands the entrance to the English Channel, with one of the finest natural harbours in the world. It is the largest conurbation in the South West peninsula with a population of more than 250,000. Although there has been occupation of the area from ancient times, the present city is a fairly recent creation. Named Sudtone in the Domesday Book, control of the town passed to Plympton, a small but busy port that exported tin. Silting up of the River Plym meant that Plympton lost its trade to Sutton (a derivation of the old name), which grew from being a small fishing village to a centre for overseas trade.

By the 14th century, the town's value as a naval base had been recognised and Sutton had become known as Plymouth, though the previous name survives today in the title of its original harbour. The port continued to develop in both size and importance, and most famously was the base for Elizabethan seafarers such as Drake and Raleigh. The Cattewater provided sheltered anchorage for ships prior to the construction of The Breakwater in Plymouth Sound, and it was here that the English Navy lay in wait for the Spanish Armada.

In 1690 work started on the Royal Dockyard in the Hamoaze, on the eastern banks of the Tamar. The original 15-acre site expanding eventually to an area of more than 900 acres, making it the principal Royal Navy Yard and the biggest dockyard in Western Europe. The new town that grew up around the yard became known as Dock, and by the 18th century it had become larger than Plymouth itself. At the beginning of the next century the population of Plymouth was 16,000, a little behind that of Exeter, the county town, while that of Dock was in excess of 23,000. The latter's name was changed to Devonport in 1824. Two decades later, the need for enhanced facilities for steamships led to a major expansion of the dockyard at Keyham.

Another town, Stonehouse, developed between Plymouth and Devonport, and the 'Three Towns' were long dominated by the Armed Forces, Stonehouse providing a home for the Royal Marines. With the advent of the First World War in 1914, the fortress commander had to liaise with three different civic bodies, so it was considered appropriate that the towns amalgamate as Plymouth, with city status being granted in 1928.

The first railway in the area was the goods-only Plymouth & Dartmoor; a horse-drawn tramroad that was built with a view to opening up Dartmoor for development. Built to a 4ft 6in gauge (which became known as the 'Dartmoor' gauge), it opened from near Princetown to Crabtree on the River Plym on 26 September 1823. Although subsequently extended, this was only ever a minor enterprise, but its existence was to figure prominently in future railway developments within Plymouth and the surrounding area, some of which are detailed in these pages.

Plymouth was not connected to the expanding national railway network until the broad-gauge South Devon Railway was extended from Totnes in 1848; its main line eventually ran from an end-on junction with the Bristol & Exeter Railway at Exeter St David's to a terminus at Plymouth Millbay. Originally envisaged by Isambard Kingdom Brunel for operation by the atmospheric system, the SDR was taken via a winding route over the southern foothills of Dartmoor, leaving an unfortunate legacy that endures today. The broad gauge continued westwards to Truro with the opening of the Cornwall Railway in 1859, both companies later amalgamating with the Great Western Railway (in 1878 and 1889 respectively).

Meanwhile standard-gauge trains reached Plymouth in 1876 when the London & South Western Railway commenced operations between London Waterloo and a terminus in Devonport, travelling via Lydford and using running powers over mixed-gauge SDR track from there to Devonport Junction. The L&SWR finally gained its own route into the 'Three Towns' after encouraging the Plymouth, Devonport & South Western Junction Railway to build an independent railway from Lydford to Devonport; this opened in 1890. The L&SWR operated all trains on the PD&SWJR's main line, and both companies became part of the Southern Railway at the 1923 'Grouping'.

Despite both the GWR and the L&SWR needing to cooperate by having running powers over sections of each other's track within the city, there was tremendous rivalry between the two workforces, with each barely acknowledging the other's existence! Both companies developed a network of branch lines in and around Plymouth, but there is an interesting contrast in these railways, with the L&SWR's branches largely urban in nature and built to serve Plymouth's maritime activities. On the other hand, the broad-gauge interests were involved in the construction of a number of what many would consider to be 'classic' GWR branches, often running through delightful rural scenery.

During the Second World War Plymouth was one of the worst bombed cities in the country; in particular seven raids in March and April 1941 reduced much of the centres of Plymouth and Devonport to rubble. The dockyards were the main targets, though in the event they were able to continue in operation. Civilian casualties were very high, however, and as we will learn the railway system was also affected.

These words are being written at a time when the news is full of references to the 50th anniversary of the publication of 'The Beeching Report'. However, most of the branch lines within this book's area and also nearly all of the intermediate stations between Plymouth and Totnes had already been closed before the release of that document. Also, the Kingsbridge branch was already under consideration for the withdrawal of its services. The only new closure proposal in the report was the line from Okehampton, and although it is probable that many of the subsequent closures could be justified, with the benefit of hindsight the loss of this section of railway has to be considered to be one of the major mistakes of the time. Although largely outside the parameters of this book, the Callington branch was also 'listed', though consent to close the section as far as Gunnislake was refused, thus also ensuring the survival of part of the ex-SR main line into Plymouth.

Apart from this branch, only the ex-GWR main line provides a passenger service today within our designated area. The manufacturing and defence sectors have always made up the backbone of Plymouth's economy, and with the decline in these activities the city has suffered deprivation. Good transport links are important in any regeneration plans, but the city lost its airport in 2011 and has no direct motorway connection. The railway is therefore still of great importance to Plymouth, and although much investment is currently being made in Britain's railways, the South West often appears to be a poor relation. Partly due to the tortuous route through South Devon, the fastest journey to London currently takes more than 3 hours on an HST. Although these have been admirable trains, they are now more than 35 years old, with no plans to replace them in the foreseeable future.

As always, I should like to record my thanks to all of the 'past' photographers for their invaluable contributions and, where applicable, the holders of various photographic collections; all are credited individually within. I am also most grateful to Mike Hunt for information, and for his comments on the manuscript.

Tavistock North to Devonport King's Road

TAVISTOCK NORTH: Wanting its own route from Lydford to Plymouth, the L&SWR encouraged the Plymouth, Devonport & South Western Junction Railway to build a 28-mile-long double-track railway, which opened to passengers on 2 June 1890. The route flanked the western side of Dartmoor before entering the ancient stannary town of Tavistock, where a station was built on the hillside above the town on the west side of the valley of the River Tavy. In about 1910 a train for Plymouth is waiting to leave; it will almost immediately cross a long stone-built viaduct. The suffix 'North' was added to the name in September 1949, post-nationalisation, when it could finally be acknowledged that the town was also served by another railway on the opposite side of the valley!

A footpath/cycleway now crosses the viaduct and a view from its northern end in November 2012 shows that housing now occupies the trackbed. Council offices have been built on the site of the goods yard, but the main station buildings survive and have been converted into three luxury holiday cottages. *Author's collection/DHM (2)*

NEAR BERE ALSTON: Just over a mile from Bere Alston station the railway passed under the Tavistock to Bere Alston road at Gawton Bridge. Exmouth Junction's 'N' Class 2-6-0 No 31857 is tackling the 1 in 75 grade as it approaches with a train from Plymouth in the spring of 1962. The lofty Calstock Viaduct, on the Callington branch, can be seen crossing the Tamar Valley in the background, 2 miles away.

Passenger services between Bere Alston and Okehampton ran for the last time on Sunday 5 May 1968. The cutting was very overgrown in 2012 but much of the trackbed is intact between Bere Alston and Tavistock. By moving a few paces to the right it was still possible to gain a clear view of Calstock Viaduct. At the time of writing there are proposals to reinstate the railway to Tavistock, with funding coming from property developers wishing to build a substantial number of houses in the town. The new terminus would, however, have to be built to the south of the original in view of the developments seen on the previous page.
Peter F. Bowles, R. Woodley collection/DHM

BERE ALSTON: The Callington branch had its origins in the 3ft 6in-gauge East Cornwall Mineral Railway; a 7½-mile line that ran from a quay on the Cornish side of the Tamar at Calstock to Kelly Bray, serving various mining activities. The 'new' branch was built by the PD&SWJ and opened on 2 March 1908, connecting with its main line at Bere Alston. The L&SWR operated all trains on the main line from the outset, but not on the branch, which remained independent until both companies became part of the Southern Railway at the 1923 'Grouping'. The last train over the final 5 miles of the branch beyond Gunnislake ran on 5 November 1966, but the remainder of the branch, together with the former main line from Bere Alston to Plymouth were retained to provide a service to a geographically remote area that has poor road access. The 1125 Plymouth to Gunnislake service is seen on 14 August 1969; although the main line beyond here had closed in the previous year, the track to Bere Alston was still double at that time and the 30-lever signal box still in use.

The track from St Budeaux was singled from 7 September 1970; the box closed at the same time, but was still standing on 6 October 2011 as No 150248 waited with the 1054 Plymouth to Gunnislake service.
R. A. Lumber/DHM

BERE ALSTON: Branch trains used the outer face of the up island platform. In a particularly busy scene on Monday 7 July 1958, Plymouth Friary's 'O2' Class 0-4-4T No 30192 is seen from the station footbridge as it awaits departure with the 3.15pm mixed train to Callington, the load comprising a Brake Composite and four vans. Meanwhile Laira's ex-GWR 2-6-0 No 6319 is pausing with the 2.25pm Friary to Exeter Central train. Some wagons can be glimpsed in the down platform; these form part of (probably) the 9.30am Yeoford to Friary goods train, hauled by Exmouth Junction-based 'Mogul' No 31846. The goods yard is to the left, with the goods shed visible beyond the end of the branch train. At one time there was a considerable interchange of traffic here, particularly with large volumes of fruit and flowers transported.

By 1968 the Tamar Valley horticultural traffic was concentrated at Saltash on the main line, with a BR carting agent hauling the traffic by road from acceptance points at Bere Alston and Calstock goods sheds; subsequently this business transferred completely to road. The station is remarkably intact, with a number of buildings still standing, including the goods shed, which is used by the 'Station Garage'. *R. A. Lumber/ DHM*

BERE ALSTON: Looking to the right of the previous scene, the main station building comes into view. This was built in granite and included the station master's house, booking hall, porters' room and ladies' room with an adjoining gents' toilet. The large village is not far to the south of the station. 'O2' 0-4-4Ts took over the Callington branch passenger duties in 1929, but they were totally replaced by Ivatt 2-6-2Ts in 1961. 'Prairie' tank No 41315 is standing with the 12.50pm to Plymouth on 1 April that year, while another of the class, No 41317, is shunting in the goods yard. Both were based at Plymouth Friary, but that depot also had a two-road wooden sub-shed at Callington that could house two engines.

Freight traffic ceased at the end of February 1966, with three remaining sidings in the goods yard being taken out of use in 1968, six months after the main line to the north was closed. From 12 August 1968 the remaining stations on the Gunnislake branch became unstaffed halts, with tickets sold by the train conductor-guard. Both this and the previous 'present' photo were taken in March 2013. (The Callington branch is covered in volume numbers 17 and 54 of this series.) *Peter W. Gray/DHM*

BERE ALSTON: Bulleid's 'light Pacifics' took over many of the SR's services west of Exeter in September 1945, and from the next year they were also used on the interchange workings over the GWR route via Newton Abbot. Those that were rebuilt from 1957 saw an increase in weight, and were banned from this route until 1960, by which time strengthening work had been undertaken on Meldon Viaduct. In about 1962 Exmouth Junction's 'West Country' 4-6-2 No 34108 *Wincanton* waits in the down platform with a train for Plymouth.

Since the route from St Budeaux was singled, Gunnislake trains have stopped at the former down platform, where they reverse before using a 'new' junction to gain access to the branch. The train crew unlock the ground frame to change the direction of the points. The footbridge had been removed, but the steps were still in situ on 24 February 1972 as Class 118 unit No P481 waits with the 1213 Gunnislake to Plymouth service.

The steps have since been demolished, and in the third view No 150248 forms the 1145 service from Gunnislake on 6 October 2011. *Peter F. Bowles, R. Woodley collection/DHM (2)*

BERE FERRERS: This station, about 2½ miles south of Bere Alston, opened with the line and serves an isolated village near the end of the Bere peninsula, on the west bank of the River Tavy. This southward-looking early-20th-century view shows the substantial buildings provided on the down side, including the station master's house. The small goods yard is largely obscured by these buildings, but the goods shed can be glimpsed above the canopy. A signal box is located on the down platform, just beyond the footbridge.

The goods yard closed in 1962 and, following the removal of two crossovers, the signal box was closed in 1968; it was subsequently removed, together with the canopy and footbridge. The station is still open, however, but the buildings and goods yard have been sold and the owner has established a collection of railway relics here. He has also erected the former L&SWR Pinhoe signal box in a different position from the original. It is complete with a frame and block instruments and bears the name Beer Ferris, the station's original spelling until 1897. No 150123 is leaving with the 1540 Plymouth to Gunnislake service on Easter Sunday, 31 March 2013. *John Smith, Terry Gough collection/DHM*

TAVY VIADUCT: About 1½ miles further south, the railway reaches the tip of the peninsula and crosses the Tavy, just before its confluence with the River Tamar, by means of the most significant engineering feature on this part of the line. The viaduct is 1,449 feet long and comprises a central section of eight bowstring girder spans supported on pairs of cast-iron cylinders; additionally, on the north side there are two masonry arches on the viaduct's approach, with another seven on the south side. The appropriately named 'West Country' 4-6-2 No 34104 *Bere Alston* is crossing with the 9.00am Waterloo to Plymouth train on 4 August 1960. This loco and the previously seen No 34108 were the last of the 'light Pacifics' to be rebuilt, both emerging from Eastleigh Works in May 1961.

Under today's Health & Safety regime it is no longer possible to stand in the late Hugh Ballantyne's footsteps. 'Sprinter' No 150248 forms the 1345 Gunnislake to Plymouth service on 15 January 2013. The branch has seen a gradual increase in use in recent years, with more than 175,000 journeys recorded in 2012. *Hugh Ballantyne, Rail Photoprints/DHM*

TAMERTON FOLIOT: After crossing the Tavy, the railway climbs through a deep cutting before reaching this station, which opened in December 1897. It was a somewhat basic affair, although a substantial building on the down side included the station master's house, a booking hall, waiting rooms and toilets; there was no goods yard. This view possibly includes the full complement of staff, with a porter in the foreground and the station master (and his wife?) behind. The photo dates from after a short-lived signal box had closed (different sources suggest that this happened in either 1911 or 1918); it had been located on the platform to the right. The occupation overbridge leads to Warleigh Wood, now a nature reserve.

At one time there was a busy seasonal traffic in rabbits and strawberries, but unfortunately not in people! The station was the least busy on the line and no doubt its location at the end of a lane, almost 2 miles from the village, contributed to this. What traffic there was suffered at the hands of bus competition and eventually in January 1959 the station became an unstaffed halt, with complete closure at the end of the summer service on Sunday 9 September 1962. The main building is now occupied privately and can be seen from the bridge on 15 January 2013 as No 150248 passes the overgrown site forming the 1254 Plymouth to Gunnislake service. *Author's collection/DHM*

TAMERTON VIADUCT: Soon after leaving Tamerton Foliot station the line crosses Tamerton Creek, firstly on an embankment constructed using the spoil excavated from the cutting on the north side of the station, then over a 117-yard-long viaduct. The creek is in the foreground, with the River Tamar beyond, as an unidentified unrebuilt 'West Country' 'Pacific' heads north with a train from Plymouth. The train has just crossed the straight stone-built Ernesettle embankment, which was constructed in 1853 to reclaim an area of salt marsh from the Tamar estuary. The Ernesettle Royal Navy Armaments Depot is located at the south end of this embankment, and has been rail-served since 1938.

The Tamerton embankment is now heavily overgrown. A 'Sprinter' forms the 1045 Bere Alston to Plymouth service on 18 November 2012; the line beyond to Gunnislake was closed for engineering work on that Sunday. The Armaments depot is still rail-connected and the sidings see occasional use, three trains operating to there in 2012. *Peter F. Bowles, R. Woodley collection/DHM*

19

ST BUDEAUX VICTORIA ROAD: St Budeaux was a separate but growing village when this station opened with the line in 1890, but nine years later it merged with the town of Devonport, eventually becoming one of Plymouth's busy suburbs. The station is situated in a cutting in a large residential district and provided a convenient commuter service for the local population, despite facing competition initially from the tram system, then from buses. There was no footbridge, and access to the platforms was gained via walkways from a road overbridge. The one on the down side was covered, and led to the station house and booking hall, which were at road level. The signal box and small goods yard were on the other side of the road bridge; the former was damaged by a bomb in 1941. The suffix 'Victoria Road' was added to the name in September 1949, and the station was unmanned from 1965. In this view from the up platform in July 1966, the substantial single-storey stone building opposite is still standing, having been occupied as waiting rooms, offices and toilets. Most of the covered walkway has been removed, but the final portion is on the right. Only a small shelter was provided on the up side.

This is the last former SR station within the city to remain open. No 150243 calls with the 0929 departure from Gunnislake to Plymouth on 19 April 2013. The branch's Train Staff is kept in a locked cabinet here, and is released when a down train occupies the station track circuit. *Bernard Mills/DHM*

FORD: In just 1½ miles from St Budeaux the line passed through two short-lived halts that had been opened in 1906 in connection with railmotor services, before entering this original 1890 station. Mostly located in a cutting, it served a large residential area inland from Devonport Dockyard, with the GWR's Ford station only about a quarter of a mile to the west. Viewed from the station footbridge, 'N' Class 2-6-0 No 31842 has just crossed Ford Viaduct as it approaches with an up train in the spring of 1962. A siding and signal box had once been located on the right, the latter closing in 1947.

The station survived until the line between St Budeaux and Devonport King's Road was closed from Monday 7 September 1964, the rationale being the high cost of maintaining the many bridges and tunnels on the route. Trains were diverted via the WR route to North Road station (see pages 30-31). Since closure the cutting has been filled in and a public park created. Housing has been erected on the southern approach to the station, but the house to the right of the 'Mogul' can also be seen in the January 2013 scene.

Peter F. Bowles, R. Woodley collection/DHM

FORD VIADUCT was a graceful structure built from concrete blocks and faced with limestone. It was 135 yards long and up to 88 feet high, with seven arches of 50-foot span. Exmouth Junction's rebuilt 'Battle of Britain' 4-6-2 No 34060 *25 Squadron* has just left Ford station and is crossing the viaduct on the same day in the spring of 1962. It will shortly enter the 363-yard-long Ford Tunnel, at the far end of which the L&SWR line passed underneath the GWR's main line; the latter also in a tunnel.

The viaduct and approach embankment were demolished in 1987, and housing has been built on the site of the latter. However, what appears to be original railway fencing survives in January 2013. The overgrown cutting leading to the tunnel can also still be viewed from the nearby Pasley Street bridge. *Peter F. Bowles, R. Woodley collection/DHM*

DEVONPORT KING'S ROAD: Another 'railmotor' halt was located in a short cutting beyond Ford Tunnel, before the line plunged into the 534-yard-long Devonport Park Tunnel. Emerging from this tunnel, the railway passed under Paradise Road and curved sharply into the L&SWR's original Plymouth terminus. This view from the road bridge includes BR Standard Class 5MT No 73044 on the 9-chain-radius curve as it leaves with the 4.52pm Plymouth to Salisbury train on Saturday 15 August 1964, just three weeks before this section of line closed completely.

The site of the station is now occupied by the City College, with gardens at this end of the property. *R. A. Lumber/DHM*

DEVONPORT KING'S ROAD station was originally named Devonport & Stonehouse when opened on 18 May 1876, referring to two of the 'Three Towns', and trains arrived from the east after running over GWR metals from Lydford. The second part of the name was soon dispensed with, however. The impressive passenger station had a glazed roof spanning four tracks and two platforms, with the main building on the departures side. An open footbridge was provided beneath the overall roof. It was converted from a terminus to a through station in 1890 when trains started to arrive via the Tavistock route; what had previously been down trains were now up ones, and vice versa.

The station was badly damaged in the 1941 blitz, the main casualty being the overall roof. One gable end survived, but this was demolished in 1945 when the Southern Railway rebuilt the station, with standard platform awnings erected. An enclosed footbridge was also provided. The suffix 'King's Road' was added to the name in September 1949 to distinguish it from the WR's Albert Road station. After the passenger service was diverted in 1964, the station reverted to its original role as a branch terminus from Devonport Junction, albeit now for goods and parcels traffic only. The yard was served once or twice daily by a freight train, usually hauled by a diesel shunter. After final closure in 1971 and subsequent demolition, the main college building was erected here. The former station approach road is a mite more congested in October 2011! *Author's collection/DHM*

DEVONPORT KING'S ROAD: This view from the iron footbridge that spanned six tracks at the east end of the station includes 70-year-old Adams 'O2' 0-4-4T No 30225 engaged in shunting duties. This loco had been allocated to Friary shed since 1954, and became WR stock following the transfer of that shed to WR control in 1958. It is thought that this photo dates from about March 1962; the loco was transferred to Eastleigh on the 26th of that month and was one of two withdrawn at the end of the year, making the class extinct on the mainland. The two tracks on the right run to the passenger station, with those on the left serving the extensive goods yard. The yard is split into two parts by the single-track Stonehouse Pool branch, which is descending at 1 in 40 to the left of the lamp post, and will run through a 101-yard-long tunnel under the substantial goods shed, the roof of which can be seen above the Paradise Road bridge. This area is now part of the college's car park. *Peter F. Bowles, R. Woodley collection/DHM*

Stonehouse Pool branch

STONEHOUSE BRIDGE: The branch name refers to a tidal creek that at one time extended up to a mile inland (see also page 42), though much of this inlet has been reclaimed at different times over the years. Stonehouse Bridge was originally a toll bridge (known locally as 'Half-penny Gate Bridge'), and carried the main Stonehouse to Devonport road over the inlet. During the Second World War the bridge was dammed, severing the connection with the creek to the south, and infilling with demolition rubble took place after the war and continued until the 1970s. After emerging from the tunnel beneath the goods shed, the branch ran on to an embankment and paralleled King's Road until it ran beneath the Devonport side of the bridge. Class 'O2' No 30183 is propelling its brake van towards the bridge on 11 September 1952; Devonport King's Road station can be glimpsed to the right of the tree behind the loco.

A footpath now follows much of the trackbed from the station site to here. Due to tree growth, a position to the right of the 'past' scene was selected; the view includes a car park located on infilled land. *Peter F. Bowles, R. Woodley collection/DHM*

RICHMOND WALK LEVEL CROSSING: The L&SWR built the goods-only branch in 1878 with the aim of developing the foreshore, but the line originally terminated just beyond Stonehouse Bridge, and it was then the responsibility of the Stonehouse Pool Improvement Company to construct the final section. Subsequently the L&SWR leased the southern section and built new quays; the extended mile-long branch was open for goods traffic in 1886. The 'South Western' also had its eyes on the GWR's Millbay ocean liner business, and an island platform was later built at the terminus. This was not a successful venture, however, and boat trains only ran from 1904 to 1910, then the station buildings were destroyed in the 1941 blitz. Class 'E1R' 0-6-2T No 32095 is on the crossing while shunting near the quays at 12.25pm on 22 April 1954.

Latterly the branch goods train only operated once or twice a week, and the line south of the crossing had already been closed by 18 June 1966 when the Plymouth Railway Circle operated its 'Plymouth Suburban' brake-van tour over the branch. D2177 is about to pass over the crossing with seven vans in tow. The tour did reach the quayside, but was unable to make it to the end of the line due to concerns over the state of the track. It has been suggested that the last goods train also ran that month, but the branch was not officially closed until May 1970, with the track lifted a year later. The October 2012 photo shows surviving rails at the site of the crossing. *Alan Lathey, Transport Treasury/M. E. Hunt/DHM*

Royal Albert Bridge to Millbay

ROYAL ALBERT BRIDGE: The River Tamar provided a formidable barrier during construction of the Cornwall Railway, acting as a natural boundary between the counties of Devon and Cornwall. Isambard Kingdom Brunel's solution to the problem was this magnificent bridge, constructed mainly of wrought iron and opened on 2 May 1859. The Tamar is 1,100 feet wide at this point, and although a ferry service was provided for road transport the railway offered easy access to and from Plymouth, with substantial numbers of commuters and shoppers carried. Steam railmotors were used on an intensive service between Saltash (on the Cornish side of the river) and Plympton from 1904, and new halts were opened in the Plymouth district, partly aimed at competing with the newly electrified tram system. A Saltash bound 'auto-train' headed by No 6420 is viewed from the signal box on 22 April 1959; the trailer is one of the more modern type recently transferred to these services from elsewhere on the Western Region.

Just two months later work started on a suspension bridge for road traffic, and when it was completed in October 1961 it was the longest such bridge in the UK. It is seen here in the following spring as 2-8-0 No 3849 approaches with an up ballast train. *Peter W. Gray/Peter F. Bowles, R. Woodley collection*

ROYAL ALBERT BRIDGE: The first signal box here opened in 1902, being required to control the junction of the newly doubled line from Keyham with the single line over the bridge. It only had a short life, however, and was replaced by a new 15-lever box just six years later when a down avoiding loop was provided on the approach to the bridge. A new 25-lever frame was installed in June 1952 to control the signals and points hitherto worked from St Budeaux West box, thus permitting the latter's closure. Soon afterwards, on a dreary 12 August 1952, 0-6-0PT No 6420 is seen again as it propels an auto-train from Saltash at 6.30pm; it is also hauling a milk tank. The ex-SR line from Tavistock runs alongside the river and passes beneath the bridge approaches between two of the seven granite piers.

The signal box closed on 2 July 1973 when the Plymouth panel's area of control was extended, and the main line was singled from just west of St Budeaux Ferry Road station. The building survives, and has been used by engineers working on the bridge. A two-year-long £11.5 million scheme to refurbish the Grade 1 listed bridge commenced in 2011; the work includes blast-cleaning to expose the original surface, the repair of any corroded areas and repainting the whole structure. The work is designed to ensure that the bridge will last for at least another century. No 150102 was recorded working the 1251 Penzance to Newton Abbot service on 16 October 2012. *Derek Frost/DHM*

ST BUDEAUX: The Southern and Great Western routes ran side-by-side here, but remained unconnected despite several proposals to link them. Eventually a wartime connection was financed by the Ministry of War Transport with the aim of providing an alternative route via the SR into the vital Devonport Dockyard. It opened on 2 March 1941, and was a timely move as it proved of immense value when Plymouth was heavily bombed in the following two months. 'O2' 0-4-4T No 30183 approaches Western Region metals after running round its transfer freight from Devonport King's Road to the dockyard at 10.15am on 11 January 1951. It has a brake-van at each end of its short train to facilitate the reversal. Prior to the opening of the connection, this daily working had to run via North Road, initially over mixed-gauge track. The WR's St Budeaux Ferry Road station is just to the left of this view, while the stock on the right is standing in sidings adjacent to the SR's main line. The St Budeaux Victoria Road goods yard is on the other side of this line.

Track in this goods yard was lifted in October 1963. The connection was upgraded for regular passenger trains during 1964 and this allowed the 7 September closure of the former SR route between St Budeaux and Devonport. The closed route was subsequently lifted, and by 22 September 1970 only the double track from St Budeaux East to Victoria Road station remained. North British Type 2 diesel-hydraulic No D6323 is seen from a Gunnislake-bound DMU as it waits for the road on to the main line with the 1607 trip from the Ernesettle Admiralty Depot to Keyham and Tavistock Junction yard.

The ex-SR route from St Budeaux Victoria Road to Bere Alston was singled from 7 September 1970, with a new facing crossover providing access to the branch. No 150232 approaches the junction with the 1345 Gunnislake to Plymouth service on 16 October 2012. The former railway land to the right has been redeveloped, part being used for road improvements. *Alan Lathey, Transport Treasury/John Medley/DHM*

As viewed from St Budeaux Ferry Road box, an auto-train from Saltash is propelled by No 6420 past the connection on 1 December 1957. The Plymouth suburban trains had a special type of paired 70-foot-long wooden-bodied trailer coaches, with end entrances and gangways to facilitate both entry and exit and ticket-issuing at the halts. The earliest were in use for more than 50 years and were very run-down by this date, the last being removed from traffic in 1958. Pending the introduction of DMUs on these services they were replaced by more modern steel-panelled trailers, which were available due to branch-line closures and dieselisation elsewhere. *Terry Nicholls*

ST BUDEAUX EAST: The wooden 17-lever signal box opened on 2 June 1916 when a short branch was provided to the Admiralty Ordnance Depot at Bull Point. The box was normally switched out, and was manned by staff from Ferry Road station when the branch trip operated. The original frame was too small to operate the revised layout when the 1941 connection to the SR was opened, but rather than build a new box its internal staircase was replaced by outside steps, thus providing additional space for the new 36-lever frame. No 30183 is about to cross over to the SR with the returning trip from Devonport Dockyard to Devonport King's Road

at 10.55am on 10 January 1951. The Bull Point branch is trailing in from the right.

The box was renamed St Budeaux Ferry Road when St Budeaux West closed on 22 June 1952, and was itself closed on 2 July 1973 when control passed to the Plymouth panel; the Bull Point branch was then operated by a ground frame. The branch connection was severed in July 1990 by removing several lengths of rail, and officially 'closed' when deleted from TOPS in May 1991, though it is likely that it had not been used for several years. In a view from a little to the west, preserved 'Black 5' 4-6-0 No 45407 *The Lancashire Fusilier* is crossing on to the Gunnislake branch with the second 'Tamar Belle' excursion on 27 March 2007, the 1Z24 1500 Plymouth to Bere Alston. *Alan Lathey, Transport Treasury/DHM*

KEYHAM JUNCTION: Pannier tank No 6400 is sandwiched between two pairs of auto-trailers as it passes the junction en route to Saltash at 12.40pm on 16 April 1960; the branch into Devonport Dockyard can be noted on the left. Beyond the bracket signal, Type 2s Nos D6318 and D6319 are crossing the 385-yard-long Weston Mill Viaduct with the Penzance to Wolverhampton Low Level 'Cornishman'. When the 53-mile-long Cornwall Railway opened from Plymouth to Truro in April 1959 there were 34 timber viaducts, with an aggregate length of about 4 miles – on no other main-line railway in the UK were there so many viaducts per mile. This was one of three on the Plymouth side of the Tamar; the present viaduct dates from 1903 when it replaced the original timber structure over Weston Mill Lake, and comprises four sets of steel bowstring girders with elaborate masonry abutments at each end.

The land beneath the viaduct has since been reclaimed. 'Sprinter' No 150123 is passing the junction forming the 1141 Penzance to Newton Abbot service on 6 October 2011; the shed on the left houses the ground frame that now controls the junction. *Peter W. Gray/DHM*

KEYHAM JUNCTION: The branch opened in June 1867, providing access to the extensive Dockyard internal system. For many years both the GWR and the L&SWR/SR ran a freight train or two each weekday into the Dockyard. The latter was usually first to arrive, and we have already seen examples of this working; here ex-GWR 0-6-0PT No 9711 is being monitored by a Dockyard policeman as it propels its train onto the down main at 4.00pm on 23 April 1957; it will then return to either Laira or Tavistock Junction yards. A security gate across the track is located immediately below the photographer's vantage point. Just beyond this is the Admiralty platform, which has been used in the past by special trains for Navy personnel.

Use of the branch gradually declined, although there was extensive traffic during the Falklands War in 1982. The last conventional freight movement occurred in 1984. Currently it is only used for the occasional movement of waste from the refitting of nuclear submarines, which is taken to the reprocessing facilities at Sellafield. Here DRS Nos 20303 and 20312 are reversing an empty flask wagon into the dockyard on 1 May 2012; increased security now comprises two men and a dog! *Alan Lathey, Transport Treasury/DHM*

KEYHAM: The 33-lever signal box opened on 25 June 1900, when the double track was extended from Keyham Viaduct East. It replaced an earlier structure, and controlled the connection between the double and single lines, the junction to the dockyard and, a couple of years later, a new goods yard. In 1937 the up passenger loop was extended to accommodate freight trains of up to 49 wagons, and a larger frame of 59 levers was installed. This almost filled the box and an outside porch was constructed to allow easier access for the signalmen. On 30 April 1941 No 4911 *Bowden Hall* suffered a direct (and fatal) hit after being brought to a stand adjacent to the box during an air raid; fortunately the crew survived, having sought shelter beneath the signal box steps. The structure became a 'fringe' box to the Plymouth panel in November 1960. On 24 February 1972 Type 2 No 7505 (later 25155) approaches with an up trip freight; it will shortly call at Keyham yard.

The box was closed on 2 July 1973 when the panel was extended, and the building was subsequently demolished. No 150233 approaches forming the 1046 Penzance to Plymouth service on 6 October 2011. *Both DHM*

KEYHAM station opened on 1 July 1900, a few days after the line from the south had been doubled. It served both the Royal Naval Barracks (now known as HMS *Drake*), which had opened in 1889 adjacent to the dockyard branch, and the considerable housing development that had grown up to serve the Naval installations in the area. Initially comprising just two platforms, a goods yard was in situ by 1903 when the line northwards was doubled. A siding to the rear of the up platform was converted into a loop in 1910. The main building was located on the down side, and is about to be passed by No D1045 *Western Viscount* with the 0830 Paddington to Penzance train on 24 February 1972.

The station is still open, but just basic shelters are provided on each platform, and only Gunnislake branch services and some peak stopping trains to and from Cornwall call today. The 0730 Paddington to Penzance service (powered by Nos 43025 and 43186) storms by on 2 October 2012. *Both DHM*

KEYHAM goods yard closed to general traffic on 19 July 1965, and the siding through the goods shed was subsequently taken out of use and lifted. The loop adjacent to the up platform was retained, however, and used in connection with movements to and from the dockyard. Another 24 February 1972 scene includes No D1033 *Western Trooper* with the 1225 Penzance to Paddington train; the loco will be changed at Plymouth.

The yard was used on a couple of occasions in 1998 for the unloading of stone trains, the aggregate being used as backfill in a fibre-optic cable-laying programme. The goods shed was demolished in about 2000 and the yard sold for housing development. The loop is, however, still in place, and preserved Stanier 5MT 4-6-0 No 45407 is seen again as it passes on 27 March 2007 with 1Z22, the 0905 Bere Alston to Plymouth Friary 'Tamar Belle' charter. *Both DHM*

FORD HALT was opened on 1 June 1904 in connection with the new railmotor service. Located about halfway between Keyham and Dockyard stations, it was initially unadvertised and intended for use by workmen. However, it was sufficiently popular that in 1906 the platforms were extended to 398 feet on the down side and 402 feet on the up, with shelters provided, and an advertised service commenced on 23 May of that year. The halt was known as 'Ford Platform' until 10 July 1922. On 23 May 1935 'Castle' Class 4-6-0 No 4090 *Dorchester Castle* passes with an up train.

The halt was staffed until 1937, and was closed from 6 October 1941 after heavy bombing damaged the platforms and destroyed much of the surrounding area. An exact facsimile is impossible today, but in this view, looking in the opposite direction, the remains of the down platform can be noted beyond the bridge girders. *H. C. Casserley/DHM*

DOCKYARD HALT was another of the 'railmotor halts', and opened on 1 June 1905. It was constructed at a cost of £557 and provided with two platforms, a 315-foot-long down one and a 260-foot one on the up side. The halt was supervised by the Devonport (later Albert Road) station master. The platforms were provided with 'pagoda'-style shelters, as illustrated in this photograph taken at 1147 on 3 October 1972, which also includes the 0935 Penzance to Plymouth service comprising a trio of three-car DMUs. The train has just crossed the 148-yard-long Keyham Viaduct. Ford Halt was located only about a quarter of a mile away, just to the near side of the cutting glimpsed in the distance.

The station is still open as a request stop, served by Gunnislake branch services and some Cornish main line stopping trains. The 1000 Penzance to Paddington HST passes its platforms on 2 October 2012. A modern shelter is now provided on the down platform, but there is neither a shelter nor even a seat on the up side. Ford Viaduct on the L&SWR route was located not far to the right of here. *R. A. Lumber/DHM*

DEVONPORT ALBERT ROAD was the Cornwall Railway's only station on the Plymouth side of the Tamar when it opened in 1859, and the width between the platforms in this view is an obvious legacy of its broad-gauge heritage. The photo was taken from the down platform and probably dates from the early 20th century. The 29-lever signal box can be noted beyond the footbridge; this replaced an earlier structure in 1899 when the line was doubled between here and Keyham Viaduct East. A small goods yard was located behind and beyond this box. The main line is curving towards the 125-yard-long Devonport Tunnel. The L&SWR route ran at right angles beneath this tunnel, emerging into a short cutting where its own Albert Road Halt was in use between 1 November 1906 and 13 January 1947. A second, larger goods yard was provided here in 1892, with access just to the east of the platforms.

The suffix 'Albert Road' was used between 1949 and 1968 to distinguish the station from the SR's King's Road facility. Track in the original goods yard was lifted between 1957 and 1964; the second yard closed in 1957 with traffic transferred first to the nearby King's Road depot, then eventually to Friary. The site was subsequently used by the S&T Department, with final track-lifting in 1970. The signal box was replaced by the Plymouth panel in November 1960. All station buildings have since been replaced by a single shelter on the down side, and a new footbridge has been provided in recent years. The 1345 Gunnislake to Plymouth service (No 150120) is stopping for a solitary passenger on 1 October 2012. *Author's collection/DHM*

DEVONPORT JUNCTION: A signal box with this name was opened in April 1876 on the north side of the line, to control the new loop line that provided a direct connection between North Road station (which opened in the following year) and the Cornwall Railway's route from Millbay; from the following month it also worked the L&SWR's line to that company's new Devonport terminus. When the maximum distance allowed between mechanically operated points and their controlling signal box was increased, a new box was built about 60 yards to the west in 1901. It was, however, another victim of the Plymouth panel in 1960, and had been demolished by March 1967, when we see 'Warship' No D808 *Centaur* heading towards North Road with a van train from Penzance. Wingfield Villas Halt had been located in the foreground on the GWR route between 1904 and 1921. The SR's rails on the right had lost their passenger service in 1964, but were retained for Devonport King's Road goods traffic until March 1971.

The track was lifted soon after closure, and on 24 February 1972 No D1010 *Western Campaigner* is passing with 7B33, the 1155 Exeter Riverside to Truro freight. The SR formation was subsequently filled in and the land is now part of the linear Stoke Damerel Park (also see page 6).

The third view shows No 150120 forming the 1454 Plymouth to Gunnislake service on 1 October 2012. *Bernard Mills/DHM (2)*

CORNWALL LOOP VIADUCT: A 'Hall' Class 4-6-0 is crossing the 131-yard-long 1876 masonry viaduct with an up goods train, and will soon pass North Road station. The rear of the train is straddling Cornwall Loop Junction. All sides of the triangle can be seen in this (probably) 1950s view, although the original route at this location, the South Devon Railway's 1849 main line to Millbay, is just out of sight in the foreground, where the turntable and a couple of sidings that ran parallel to this route can just be noted; these were provided in 1913 to save having to send locos to Laira for turning during busy periods. On the left, the Cornwall Railway's 1859 line crosses the curving Stonehouse Pool Viaduct. The initial structure was the only one of Brunel's CR timber viaducts built to carry double broad-gauge track, and in 1908 was the last of the original CR main line viaducts to be reconstructed.

The CR route was the first to close (16 January 1964), and the line from North Road to Millbay suffered a similar fate in 1971. The land in the foreground has since been infilled, with a dog-walking area created. Tree growth now obscures the 'past' scene, but a small gap in the undergrowth allowed a view of No 150244 crossing the viaduct as the 1145 Gunnislake to Plymouth service on 1 October 2012. The brick piers of Stonehouse Pool Viaduct survive, and since 1990 have been surmounted by a steel structure titled *Moor*, which is apparently described as an art installation... *J. T. Whitnall, Derek Frost collection/DHM*

MILLBAY: On Saturday 3 June 1961 the Plymouth Railway Circle ran a railtour from Friary, which first visited Sutton Harbour before heading for Millbay Docks. Here, on the return trip, ex-GWR 0-6-0ST No 1363 is approaching Cornwall Junction with six BR 20-ton brake-vans carrying about 60 'gricers'. The loco is a 1910 Churchward design for dock shunting that was based on a fleet of Sharp Stewart locos built for the Cornwall Mineral Railway. Laira shed once had four of the five engines that formed the class, but by 1961 No 1363 was the last survivor in the area, and acted as a back-up to the Class 03 diesel shunters used in Millbay Docks. The 39-lever junction signal box is just out of view to the left, but had been replaced by the Plymouth panel in the previous November. The building beyond the train is the Harwell Street carriage shed. Millbay's engine shed had been situated away to the right, but this closed in 1931 when Laira shed was extended. From 1958 to 1964 the Belmont Street DMU depot was located here until its function was taken over by Laira Diesel Depot.

All the track in this area was taken out of use on 14 December 1969 except for the up and down lines to the docks, but these were also closed in 1971. The whole area has since been redeveloped, with the Cornwall Junction cutting filled in. The saddle tank was preserved by the Great Western Society and left Laira for Totnes under its own steam in August 1964; it is now based at the GWS's Didcot depot. *Peter F. Bowles, R. Woodley collection/DHM*

43

MILLBAY: The South Devon Railway reached its Plymouth terminus on 2 April 1849 when its route was extended from a temporary terminus at Laira Green. The station was also used by the Cornwall Railway when it opened on 2 May 1859, but this meant that arrangements in Plymouth were far from satisfactory, with through services between the two broad-gauge systems having to reverse at Millbay. This problem was not resolved until the 'Cornwall Loop' was opened in 1876. Although of inferior quality, this historic photo is of great interest as it depicts the very last broad-gauge train from Paddington to Penzance waiting to leave on Friday 20 May 1892. The 'Cornishman' was scheduled to leave London at 10.15am and did not normally call at Millbay. The massive building in the background is the Duke of Cornwall Hotel, which was built to the Gothic style in 1865; Plymouth's first luxury hotel, it was designed to cater for travellers, being close to both the station and the docks.

The worst raids in the blitz took place in April 1941, when Millbay was badly damaged. The goods depot was destroyed and the passenger station was prematurely closed from the 23rd of that month so that it could be used for goods traffic. Its two island platforms were demolished when the site was converted for carriage sidings in 1959; this activity ceased in 1969 when carriage stabling was moved to Laira. The site was cleared and is now occupied by the Plymouth Pavilions leisure complex, but the hotel survives and can be noted in this 2011 view. *Author's collection/DHM*

MILLBAY CROSSING: A double-track line ran along the west side of Millbay station and entered the docks area after crossing Millbay Road. A 14-lever signal box was provided at this crossing in about 1898. The crossing gates overlapped each other when closed to the railway, as the road was much wider than the line. A footbridge was also located here, which provides the vantage point for our view of double-headed 4-6-0s Nos 7824 *Ilford Manor* and 7033 *Hartlebury Castle* as they leave the docks with a boat train for London, carrying passengers from the SS *Antilles* at 8.15am on 1 May 1954. The *Antilles* was a cruise ship built for the French Line (CGT), and had made its maiden voyage the previous year. It met an unhappy end after striking a reef off the island of Mustique in 1971.

French Line vessels ceased to call at the end of 1961, severing an 80-year connection with the port. The box was reduced in status from block post to ground frame on 17 March 1968, and closed when the docks line was taken out of use on 26 September 1971. *Alan Lathey, Transport Treasury/DHM*

MILLBAY DOCKS: A natural inlet that had long served as a harbour, the area was only properly developed after the Great Western Dock Co was incorporated in 1846 with a view to providing improved facilities. The South Devon, Great Western and Bristol & Exeter railways all subscribed to this company and almost inevitably the engineer for this venture was a certain I. K. Brunel. The railway was extended from Millbay station into the docks in 1850 and, after customs facilities were provided, the port was recognised as a mail packet station. Further developments included building a second pier and the provision of a floating pontoon. An inner basin was opened in 1857; it had dock gates and a dry dock on its western side. On 28 March 1959 0-6-0ST No 1363 is entering the docks and approaching East Quay with a transfer freight.

From the 1950s the amount of freight handled declined, although considerable perishable traffic from France and Spain was imported for a period in the early 1960s. Much of the quayside is now awaiting

redevelopment, including plans for a yachting marina in the inner basin. Some trackwork could still be seen in 2012; the rails running to the left in the 'past' photo will shortly form part of a diamond crossing, and this is illustrated here. *Peter F. Bowles, R. Woodley collection/ DHM*

MILLBAY DOCKS: Also on 28 March 1959, 'large Prairie' No 5143 is engaged in shunting boat train stock on the East Quay. The Ocean Terminal is in the right distance, beyond Trinity Pier, which is just visible on the extreme right. Millbay became a popular calling point for transatlantic liners; passengers could save a day from their travelling time by disembarking here and catching a fast train to London. The liners did not actually enter the docks – passengers and mail were transferred to railway-owned tenders, which brought them to land. More than six million passengers used Millbay during the 20th century; the peak year for liner traffic was 1930, when 38,472 passengers were landed from 684 vessels. This business was sufficiently lucrative that, after a brief experiment with Pullman stock, the GWR introduced eight 'Super Saloons' in 1931/32 specifically for these trains. Liner traffic declined thereafter, however, particularly after Southampton was modernised in 1934, and also with the growth in air travel after the Second World War. In 1958 172 liners called, but the numbers continued to diminish and the last special boat trains ran in 1962.

Some housing has been built on East Quay, and Brittany Ferries has operated ferry services to France and Spain from West Quay since 1973. *Peter F. Bowles, R. Woodley collection/DHM*

North Road to Laira Junction

PLYMOUTH NORTH ROAD: Standard-gauge L&SWR trains first reached the city on 18 May 1876 by accessing the GWR's Launceston branch at Lydford; mixed-gauge track was provided on the latter's route via Tavistock Junction and Laira to enable the L&SWR to reach its own terminus at Devonport. The centrally located joint station at North Road was planned to cater for both railway's services. It was largely constructed in timber to ensure rapid completion, but delays during building meant that it was not ready for use until 28 March 1877. Both companies' trains from London thus arrived from the east, but this changed from 2 June 1890 when the L&SWR began using its own route from the west; its trains terminated at North Road until the following year, when they were extended to the company's new terminus at Friary. Prior to the opening of North Road, Millbay station had been known simply as 'Plymouth', but was renamed from 1 May 1877. North Road may have been built on the cheap, but it certainly wasn't cheerful and earned a reputation for being a rather gloomy place, an image not helped in the first view, which appears to have been taken on a particularly wet day!

The second photo probably dates from early in 1961 when rebuilding work was in progress, while the 'present' frontage was recorded in October 2012. *Author's collection/M. E. Hunt collection/DHM*

PLYMOUTH NORTH ROAD: There were only two through platforms until the station was enlarged in 1908, reconstruction bringing four through platforms with six platform faces, a bay and a goods dock. Two new East and West signal boxes were also provided, containing 48 and 59 levers respectively. This expansion was necessary in part due to the success of the new suburban services, and the introduction of several direct trains from North Road to Cornwall. Further rebuilding work began in 1937, and West box was moved northwards to a new position in January 1938; a new road bridge capable of carrying four tracks was also constructed at the west end of the station. On 30 August 1958 4-6-0 No 4936 *Kinlet Hall* and 2-6-0 No 6319 are about to pass West box as they arrive at 10.40am with the 8.15am Perranporth to Paddington train. The original and smaller 1876 signal box had been located on the opposite side of the tracks.

The box was replaced by the Plymouth panel from 26 November 1960. On 10 October 2011 the 0844 Penzance to Paddington HST (power cars Nos 43091 and 43163) is arriving. *Peter W. Gray/DHM*

PLYMOUTH NORTH ROAD: Despite earlier improvements, the timber structure was still not appropriate as the city's main station, and the 1930s scheme included plans for seven through platforms with extensive new buildings. Track and signalling alterations were completed, particularly on the up side, where a new island platform (Platforms 7 and 8) was provided, but further progress was halted by the outbreak of war. On Monday 27 August 1962 North British Type 4 'Warship' No D844 *Spartan* is standing at Platform 4 with 1C33, the 11.30am Paddington to Falmouth train. It will be followed by the occupant of Platform 5, 4-6-0 No 1006 *County of Cornwall*, which is hauling the 3.46pm from Plymouth to Penzance. Meanwhile North British Type 2 No D6343 is running light engine to Millbay. The pre-war work had included the demolition of the buildings and roof coverings on the old up platform (Platforms 5 and 6), leaving the platform devoid of any shelter until the redevelopment work could be resumed.

With the closure of Friary station to passenger traffic on 15 September 1958, Southern Region services also terminated here and the suffix 'North Road' was dropped from the station title as it was now the only major station in the city. With the opening of the Plymouth panel in 1960, all lines are available for reversible running. No 43026 is on the rear of the 1657 departure to Paddington on 1 October 2012. The panel is located in a building at the west end of the former Platform 2 where it was built on part of the site of the old parcels depot. *Derek Frost/ DHM*

PLYMOUTH NORTH ROAD: Rebuilding of the station recommenced in 1956 when work was mostly concerned with the down side. The old station buildings on this side included offices for certain operating departments and alternative accommodation had to be found for these before the structure could be demolished; this part of the work commenced in May 1958. Reconstruction progressed from west to east, and buildings west of the subway were brought into use in 1960. These are to the right of this view from Platform No 3 of Ivatt 2-6-2T No 41302, which is standing at Platform 2 on Saturday 29 April 1961 with the 1.18pm departure to Tavistock North. The station is now dominated by a 10-storey office block, which is under construction.

The track layout was rationalised in 1973/74 when these two platforms ceased to have through roads; a covered dividing partition was constructed to provide both easy access for Royal Mail traffic to the docks on the east side of the station, and a walkway for passengers using Platforms 3 and 4. No 153370 is stabled in the former Platform 2, now Dock No 4, on 6 October 2011. During 2012 the canopy on the right was removed (see the cover photograph). *Derek Frost/DHM*

PLYMOUTH NORTH ROAD: The Saltash suburban services operated for more than 60 years. Initially the trains ran mainly to Plympton, with some going to Millbay. Subsequently certain trains to the west ran as far as Doublebois and even Bodmin Road. At first the service was operated by just two sets, each comprising a steam railmotor and a trailer, but such was their success that in 1909 they were supplemented with two auto-tanks and four new trailers. Additional locos and trailers arrived, and the two railmotors were rebuilt as trailers in 1920. The exclusive use of auto-operated stock on the Plymouth suburban services was unique on the GWR. The peak of intensity was just before 1930, when ten sets of coaches were in use each day; thereafter the service suffered from tram and bus competition. The services were the preserve of the '6400' Class pannier tanks from their introduction in 1932 until the end of steam; eight of the class were allocated to Laira when new. They usually operated with two auto-trailers, but during peak periods four coaches could be used, two in front of the engine and two behind. Materials for station rebuilding work can be noted on Platform 6 as No 6414 awaits departure with a Saltash train at 8.00pm on a sunny Monday 7 July 1958.

Class 118 DMUs were used on these services from Monday 13 June 1960, the start of the summer timetable; this was one of the first uses of this type of train in Devon. Steam remained on two daily trips that were continuations of Tavistock trains, and also continued to substitute for unavailable units for a further couple of years. Patronage from Cornwall was to suffer with the opening of the Tamar road bridge in April 1962, and the service finished ten years later. In the 'present' scene No 153373 has arrived in Platform 6 as the 1605 service from Exeter St David's on 1 October 2012. *R. A. Lumber/ DHM*

PLYMOUTH NORTH ROAD: Viewed from the east end of Platform 5 at 7.23pm on Saturday 29 April 1961, ex-GWR 2-6-2T No 5541 is approaching Platform 3 with the 5.40pm Launceston to Plymouth train. Traditionally Southern Region up departures also used the latter platform. An anomaly in the rebuilt station was the absence of a Platform 1. This had been envisaged in the pre-war plan as a down bay platform for Tavistock motor-trains, but the idea was abandoned when the decision was made to build a new parcels depot on the site, which included a loading dock (No 1) in place of the proposed passenger platform.

No 5541 is now preserved on the Dean Forest Railway. As previously mentioned, Platforms 2 and 3 ceased to be through ones when the track layout was rationalised during the winter of 1973/74, and at this end of the station the new bays were designated Dock Nos 2 and 3, and formed part of the parcels depot. On 1 October 2012 power car No 43125 is leading the 1406 Paddington to Penzance HST as it approaches Platform 4. *Derek Frost/DHM*

PLYMOUTH NORTH ROAD: Pannier tank No 6417 is standing at the end of Platform 8 on 11 April 1952; the station's third 'East' signal box can be glimpsed beyond the loco's bunker. Further on is the concrete Houndiscombe Bridge, which replaced a stone arch bridge in 1938; the wider structure enabled the new engine sidings to be laid, partly on the site of Mutley station's up platform. The first box had opened in 1876 as part of the development of the then new station, but was replaced by a new 48-lever structure when the station was enlarged in 1908. The third box was erected a little to the east of its predecessor and contained a 175-lever frame, later increased to 185 levers. It was brought into use on 25 June 1939 as part of the planned redevelopment of the station. With the advent of war and delay in completing the planned new layout, there were actually more spare than working levers, with many spaces in the frame where no lever was actually provided.

'Voyager' No 221131 forms the terminating 0632 service from Dundee on 1 October 2012. *Rail Photoprints Collection/DHM*

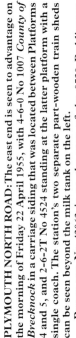

PLYMOUTH NORTH ROAD: The east end is seen to advantage on the morning of Friday 22 April 1955, with 4-6-0 No 1007 *County of Brecknock* in a carriage siding that was located between Platforms 4 and 5, and 2-6-2T No 4524 standing at the latter platform with a single coach. The station's two separate part-wooden train sheds can be seen beyond the milk tank on the left.

Power car No 43063 is on the rear of the 0730 Paddington to Penzance train as it arrives in Platform No 4 on 1 October 2012. The carriage siding was converted into a through road as part of the 1950s changes. Nos 2 and 3 Docks are on the left, now deserted following the loss of Royal Mail traffic in 2004. Beyond these the 10-storey office block of glass and concrete is prominent. It was designed to be home to what proved to be a fairly short-lived Plymouth Division, and completed in time for Dr Richard Beeching's visit to formally open the rebuilt station on 26 March 1962, some 24 years after the work had commenced! The six-year-long 'second phase' was estimated to have cost £1.8 million, although this sum also included the re-signalling, and a new diesel depot. *Peter F Bowles, R. Woodley collection/DHM*

PLYMOUTH NORTH ROAD: Viewed from the Houndiscombe Bridge, 'Britannia' Class 'Pacific' No 70024 *Vulcan* is about to pass the East signal box as it leaves with the 7.30am Truro to Paddington service on 22 April 1955.

At the end of the Second World War there were 31 mechanical signal boxes within the Plymouth area, but some were subsequently closed when either they were no longer required or their functions were incorporated into the work of adjoining boxes. North Road East closed on 26 November 1960, one of six to be lost with the introduction of the new Plymouth panel with its multiple-aspect colour-light signalling and power-operated points; it was the first box on the Western Region to be fitted with four-character train describers. Twelve more boxes closed in the next decade, mainly due to line closures or the loss of passenger services, and by 1973 there were only eight mechanical boxes in the Plymouth area. These were then closed when the control area of the panel was extended, with Totnes and St Germans becoming the 'fringe boxes'.

The long-closed North Road East signal box was still standing on 24 February 1972 when 'Peak' No 26 (later 45020) departed with 4M05, the 1250 Penzance to Crewe perishables, but has since been demolished. We can also view the 'pre-rationalisation' track layout.

The third scene illustrates the post-1973/74 set-up, and includes 'The Cornish Riviera', the 0844 Penzance to Paddington service, leaving on 1 October 2012 powered by Nos 43027 and 43130. Plymouth's power box is now among the oldest in the country, but is due to survive until 2022 under current Network Rail plans. By 2026 the entire route between Paddington and Penzance is scheduled to be controlled from the Thames Valley signalling control centre in Didcot. *Peter F. Bowles, R. Woodley collection/DHM (2)*

MUTLEY: This district is one of Plymouth's main commercial areas with a major road, Mutley Plain, running through its heart. With its terminus at Millbay not particularly central to the city, the South Devon Railway elected to build a station here, situated in a cutting and adjacent to the slightly curving 183-yard-long Mutley Tunnel. It was opened on 1 August 1871, and soon proved to be a success, becoming known as 'the gentry's station' on account of a well-heeled clientele. However, its restricted site limited the possibility of expansion and, with the need for more facilities, the joint station at North Road was opened less than six years later and a mere quarter of a mile to the west. Despite this, ticket sales, particularly for local trips, held up well and indeed at times exceeded its larger neighbour. The first photo, from the up platform, probably dates from the early years of the 20th century, and shows the substantial buildings that were provided. A signal box was located beyond the booking office/waiting rooms on the left and was in use from 1894 until it closed in 1908 as part of the changes to North Road in that year. An up train is signalled, with the grey limestone face of the tunnel visible in the distance. Mutley Plain runs over the tunnel; the large building is the rear of Mutley Baptist Church.

Business had fallen by the 1930s and, in anticipation of the major redevelopment of North Road, the station was closed on 3 July 1939. The second view from the Houndiscombe Bridge probably dates from soon after and shows that part of the up platform has been demolished, with one of two new engine spurs in place.

The third view from a passing train on 29 August 1945 includes the still standing but derelict main station building, and also shows that much of the up platform has gone.

The new sidings were used to hold engines waiting to back into North Road for up trains. They were extended in 1956, and can be noted in the foreground of the fourth picture as 4-6-0s Nos 7820 *Dinmore Manor* (now preserved) and 6025 *King Henry III* approach North Road with the down 'Cornish Riviera Express' from Paddington to Penzance on 14 June 1959. The South Devon's route from Newton Abbot to Plymouth runs through hilly terrain, with tight curves and several steep gradients up to a maximum of 1 in 37. These deficiencies are a result of both financial stringencies during the building period and Brunel's over-optimistic faith in the atmospheric system. It meant that many trains required assistance between the two towns, freight trains being banked in the rear up the major climbs, usually by a large 2-6-2T, while passenger trains normally had a pilot throughout. Passenger train assistance was one of the last tasks of the 'Bulldog' 4-4-0s, but by the 1950s both Laira and Newton Abbot sheds maintained a stud of 'Manor' Class locos, one of their main duties being their use as pilots over the banks. *Author's collection (2)/H. C. Casserley/ Terry Nicholls*

MUTLEY: Brush Type 4 No 1566 (later 47449, and now preserved on the Llangollen Railway) passes the site of Mutley station with 1V73, the 0911 Liverpool Lime Street to Plymouth train, on 24 February 1972. The colour-light signal was installed in 1960 for the Plymouth multiple-aspect signalling scheme.

The signal and one of the sidings were removed as part of the 1973/74 track rationalisation in Plymouth station. Apart from the inevitable lineside growth, the other obvious change here is the appearance of a car park that has been constructed over the railway at this end of the tunnel. The use of Class 47s on cross-country trains ended in 2002, and 'Voyager' No 220007 is forming the 0601 Glasgow Central to Plymouth service on 6 October 2011. It has just crossed from the down to the up main line in order to terminate in Platform No 8. *Both DHM*

MUTLEY: The site of the station is viewed from the cutting on the approach to Mutley Tunnel on Thursday 20 September 1962. Pannier tank No 6430 (another preserved engine, now based on the Llangollen Railway) is working the 2.10pm Plymouth to Tavistock South train. The overgrown pathway on the left formerly led to Mutley's down platform; the large building in the background is the Royal Eye Infirmary.

'Super Voyager' (an oxymoron?) No 221141, forming the 1125 Plymouth to Dundee service, is glimpsed as it is about to pass beneath the car park on 1 October 2012. Although it closed in January 2013, the Eye Infirmary building still stands, but is hidden by the undergrowth. *Derek Frost/DHM*

PLYMOUTH NO 1 CURVE: Lipson Junction, about 1¼ miles from Mutley, was created when the GWR constructed a spur from its main line to a connection with its Sutton Harbour branch at Mount Gould Junction, thus enabling L&SWR trains access to that company's new terminus at Friary. The spur opened in April 1891 in time for Friary's opening in the following July. Pannier tank No 6420 is sandwiched between four auto-coaches on the curve on 2 May 1959 while working the RCTS 'Plymouth District Rail Tour' en route to Friary; it will shortly enter a deep cutting before reaching Mount Gould Junction. Laira engine shed can be noted in the background; the building to the left is the four-road straight 'New Shed' added in 1931; by this date it was being used to house new diesels pending the construction of a purpose-built diesel depot nearby. One of the five D600 series 'Warship' Type 4s is on shed, with another at the junction with the curving 'Speedway', just beyond the second coach of the special; this line was installed in 1931 to provide a new exit from the shed and forms part of a triangle that can be used for turning locos. Laira marshalling yards are out of view to the right. The curve is still in use, but only just visible on 21 July 2012. *Peter W. Gray/DHM*

LAIRA SHED: With expansion of the cramped Millbay shed site difficult, the GWR decided to relocate its main Plymouth depot to Laira on the eastern outskirts of the city, within the triangle of lines mentioned opposite and on land that had been reclaimed from the River Plym over the years. The shed opened in 1901 and comprised a single roundhouse with 28 roads around its turntable, the 1931 shed being built alongside. At its peak the depot had an allocation of around 100 locos, ranging from the mighty 'Kings' to humble dock tanks. This photo from 22 April 1962 includes a typical line-up of locos that could be seen latterly, including 4-6-0s Nos 1004 *County of Somerset*, 5065 *Newport Castle*, 5024 *Carew Castle*, three unidentified 'Halls' and 2-6-2T No 4561. The coaling stage is immediately to the left, with a hoist in the background; the roundhouse is beyond this. The shed's District depot was Newton Abbot, and Laira was coded 83D in BR days. A 'railmotor' halt was located on the main line to the north of the depot between 1 June 1904 and 7 July 1930.

The shed closed to steam in May 1964, and totally from the next year. Demolition commenced in 1966 to make way for a staff car park and Lipson sidings; the latter are seen here from a railtour traversing the 'Speedway' on 28 May 2011. *Terry Nicholls/DHM*

LAIRA DIESEL DEPOT: It was decided in the early days of modernisation planning in the 1950s that the West of England would be one of the first areas to abandon steam. This was the first new diesel maintenance facility to be built within the WR and occupies the site formerly used as Laira Marshalling Yard. The depot was equipped for the maintenance of all diesel locomotives and diesel multiple units (DMUs) allocated to Laira and subsidiary depots in Devon and Cornwall, and is seen here under construction on 29 August 1961; part of the depot was in use by the end of that year. The three-road building on the left is the servicing shed; each track could accommodate two locos under cover and was provided with an inspection pit. The main building is the six-road maintenance shed with the main workshop of two tracks built higher to accommodate a 10-ton electric crane. The next three roads were used mainly for servicing DMUs and for the routine examination of locomotives. The track on the right was equipped with a wheel-turning lathe for re-profiling wheel tyres.

Initially the depot was associated with the WR's unique fleet of diesel-hydraulic locomotives, and a number of 'Warships' and 'Westerns' are in view on 20 April 1970; from left to right they are Nos 855 *Triumph*, 1021 *Western Cavalier*, 838 *Rapid* and 1010 *Western Campaigner*. *R. C. Riley/John Medley*

LAIRA JUNCTION: No 6833 *Calcot Grange* pilots No 6004 *King George III* past the 116-lever signal box with the 12.05 Plymouth to Paddington train on 6 August 1959. The train is about to pass over the boarded crossing of the 4ft 6in-gauge horse-worked Plymouth & Dartmoor Railway/Lee Moor Tramway. Laira shed's coal stage is prominent in the background, but the marshalling yard (beyond the signal box) had been closed in the previous December, with the up sidings already lifted to allow preparatory work on the new diesel depot. Two auto-coaches stand in the carriage sidings on the right.

The tramway across the main lines was lifted in 1960, the carriage sidings were taken out of use in 1963, and the signal box closed in November 1973. The depot's servicing shed was demolished in 1979 and replaced by a three-road HST Maintenance and Servicing Shed. A further extension was later added alongside this shed in anticipation of European Passenger Services' ill-fated 'Night Star' project. When BR introduced sectorisation, the depot became a dedicated InterCity facility, and continues to maintain a portion of First Great Western's HST fleet. Two power cars stand outside the 'new' shed as the 1135 Paddington to Plymouth service passes on 21 July 2012. *Peter W. Gray/DHM*

LAIRA JUNCTION: The name Laira originally applied to that part of the tidal estuary of the River Plym from the Cattewater up to Marsh Mills. An embankment was built between 1802 and 1809, creating a new western shoreline for the Plym and a level route into Plymouth. A toll road was built on the embankment with tolls being collected until 1924. The Plymouth & Dartmoor Railway also made use of the protection afforded by the embankment when extending its line to Sutton Harbour in 1825. The large railway site comprising the 'Laira triangle' was built on reclaimed land to the west of the embankment, an area formerly known as Lipson Lake. When the South Devon Railway built its line to Plymouth, its approach to the embankment was over a causeway. Turning in the opposite direction from the previous views, we see 0-6-0PT No 4679 approaching the junction with a transfer goods from Tavistock Junction Yard at 6.05pm on 29 April 1961. The Plym is on the right with a tidal creek in the foreground; the P&DR's route ran to the left of this inlet.

The 23 April 1970 view includes D1022 *Western Sentinel* with the 0830 Paddington to Penzance train. *Peter W. Gray/John Medley*

LAIRA JUNCTION: At the same location, but viewed from the east side of the line, an unidentified '49XX' series 'Hall' Class 4-6-0 approaches on the down main with a parcels train. The track on the right provides access to Laira Marshalling Yard, while the stored stock in the distance is in Ocean Siding, adjacent to the shore. When the South Devon Railway was extended from Totnes, its initial services ran only as far as a temporary terminus at Laira Green, well outside what was then the boundary of Plymouth. One of the reasons for this was the delay in agreeing terms with the owners of the Plymouth & Dartmoor for the sale of their route within Plymouth, as authorised by the SDR's 1846 Act; as a result the 'newcomer' was unable to cross the mineral line. It is thought therefore that Laira Green must be within the area of this photograph.

The inlet to the left has been reclaimed, and a dual carriageway built across it in the mid-1970s. GBRf No 66720 heads for Plymouth station with the stock of that company's staff special on 21 July 2012. The train has been turned using the 'Laira triangle' so that preserved No 50044 *Exeter*, at the far end of the train, will lead on the return journey to Cardiff. *Peter F. Bowles, R. Woodley collection/DHM*

Mount Gould Junction to Friary

MOUNT GOULD JUNCTION: Looking north from Lanhydrock Road, a '4500' Class 2-6-2T provides the power for a transfer goods from Laira Yard to Friary in the mid-1950s. The 31-lever signal box can be glimpsed in the right background, with Plymouth No 1 Curve emerging from the cutting just to the left of the bracket signal. The box opened in 1891 to control the junction of this curve and the GWR's Laira to Sutton Harbour branch. The two tracks in the centre foreground comprise Plymouth No 2 Curve, constructed in 1898 to allow GWR trains to access the company's Yealmpton branch. The Lee Moor Tramway's 4ft 6in-gauge line, in-filled with earth to provide a path for horses, runs parallel to the Sutton Harbour route and crosses No 2 Curve on the level.

No 2 Curve closed on 15 September 1958 and the track was lifted just 12 days later. The signal box gained a new 45-lever frame in 1959 in association with the redevelopment of Laira Yard, additional levers being used in 1960 when it became a fringe box to the Plymouth panel. From the other end of the road bridge, we see 'N' Class 2-6-0 No 31855 heading for Friary with the empty stock of the 3.22pm Okehampton to Plymouth train on 29 April 1961; note that the increasingly overgrown Lee Moor tracks are still in place. Within two months the new Laira carriage sidings were brought into use and stock stabling at Friary ended.

The Lee Moor Tramway carried china clay to Martin's Wharf until the wharf was requisitioned during the Second World War, after which the tracks saw occasional use for the conveyance of gravel from Marsh Mills to a concrete works on the Embankment, primarily to maintain the right to cross the main line at Laira. The last such working to be recorded occurred in August 1960, and the track on this part of the tramway was removed in 1962. Subsequently an unusual feature of this location was the installation in 1969 of a carriage washing plant on the down main; a switch was provided in the signal box to operate the machinery,

and care had to be taken to ensure that it was switched off before signalling a freight train through! BR Type 2 No 7577 (later 25227) is on a trip working to Friary Yard at 1600 on 14 October 1971.

The signal box closed in 1973 and the down main is now reserved for cleaning HST sets. Any trains for Friary now use the former up main, which is signalled for reversible operation. Shunter No 09013 is heading away from the camera with a scrap train from the Cattewater branch on 27 March 2007. *Peter F. Bowles, R. Woodley collection/Derek Frost/R. A. Lumber/DHM*

FRIARY JUNCTION: The GWR brought this 21-lever signal box into use in about 1895 when it replaced an earlier installation known as Tothill Crossing. It controlled the junction of the lines to Sutton Harbour and Friary. The Southern Railway took over the working of the box from August 1938. It was then manned by a Porter Signalman from Friary station, and only operational for three short periods each day, sufficient to permit the running of the twice-daily trains from Laira Yard to Sutton Harbour. The box closed on 29 September 1959, after which the entrance to the Sutton Harbour Branch was controlled by a ground frame. Shortly before that date, 'T9' No 30717 is seen from Lanhydrock Road bridge while working empty stock from Friary to Plymouth station. This will possibly form the 10.02am departure to Waterloo, the city's portion of the 'Atlantic Coast Express', which the 'Greyhound' will haul as far as Okehampton. From Friary Junction all L&SWR/SR trains traversed GWR metals as far as Devonport Junction. Plymouth No 2 Curve, by now closed, was to the left of this view; the former Mount Gould & Tothill Halt was located on this spur, adjacent to the road bridge, between 1905 and 1918. The Lee Moor Tramway can be seen running between the building and fence in the foreground; the aforementioned concrete works was located to the left, about level with Friary Junction. Both the tramway to Martin's Wharf and the Sutton Harbour branch run beneath the lattice girder bridge (top left), which carries the branch to Cattewater, Plymstock and beyond. Lucas Terrace Halt can be glimpsed on this latter route above the first coach behind the 'Greyhound'. A little further to the right, steam is rising above Friary engine shed.

70

The 16 October 2012 scene includes an additional carriage washing plant. *Peter F. Bowles, R. Woodley collection/DHM*

LUCAS TERRACE HALT comprises a single platform, faced in concrete, and was opened in October 1905 on the Turnchapel branch. It was located on an embankment about a quarter of a mile from the junction with the main line; the latter runs parallel with the branch at this point, but at a lower level out of view on the right. The platform, which was extended at its west end in 1923, was provided with a basic precast concrete shelter. Access was by steps at the east end of the shelter, with a steep path leading down to Lucas Terrace. The three-road Friary engine shed can be noted in the right background; this was the L&SWR's main depot in Plymouth. It was fully operational by 1908, when it replaced a small shed adjacent to Friary station and another older one at Devonport. The coal stage can be noted behind and just to the right of the halt's shelter.

The halt closed when the Turnchapel passenger service ended in 1951. The shed closed in May 1963 when its men, equipment and remaining locos were transferred to Laira depot. The second view shows the platform on 20 January 1983; a rail-served fertiliser distribution warehouse occupies the site of the shed. *John Smith, Terry Gough collection/DHM*

LUCAS TERRACE HALT: This view from the west end of the platform affords a clearer view of the relationship between the two routes as 'T9' 4-4-0 No 30717 descends the grade towards Friary Junction with a train for Waterloo at 2.25pm on 10 August 1951; an 'M7' 0-4-4T is next to the engine shed. A 50-foot turntable was positioned just to the left of the platform; when the Bulleid 'Pacifics' started working to Plymouth, they were too large for this turntable, and had to be turned by using the triangle via Cattewater and Friary Junctions. In the 1950s the depot usually had an allocation of more than 20 locos, ranging in size from Class 'B4' 0-4-0Ts to a small stud of the aforementioned 4-6-2s. Its BR code was 72D, but this was changed to 83H in 1958 when the shed was transferred to the Western Region.

The platform still survives, but is now heavily overgrown; by peering over a palisade fence on 3 May 2012, it was possible to record DRS Nos 37604 and 37259 'top-and-tailing' a Network Rail Radio Survey Train on the climb towards Friary. The shed site has now been further redeveloped for housing. *Alan Lathey, Transport Treasury/DHM*

FRIARY YARD: After first reaching Plymouth, the L&SWR opened a goods branch to Friary in 1878; it was served from its Devonport terminus, with a reversal at Laira Junction. Part of the goods yard can be seen in this 1926 view. The approach to the passenger station is on the right beyond the stabled coaching stock; the terminus is beyond the Tothill Road bridge (which provides the vantage point for the photos on pages 75-77). A tender-first 'T9' 4-4-0 is near the centre of the picture, possibly acting as station pilot. The walled single track in the foreground is a branch to the North Quay of Sutton Harbour, where it connected with the GWR's branch. This line, which opened in 1879, descended steeply, and will soon pass through a 74-yard-long tunnel.

The North Quay branch was closed in November 1950 as it duplicated the ex-GWR line; its cutting was subsequently filled in to provide more room in the goods yard. Friary station was closed to passengers in 1958 with a view to providing a central goods depot for Plymouth; freight traffic was transferred from Millbay and the two Devonport stations. The yard also handled Freightliner business from 1966 to July 1970, but this ended due to insufficient demand. Its status as Plymouth's main goods facility was further enhanced, however, when Tavistock Junction marshalling yard closed in January 1971. It was still a full-load freight yard and the location of a TOPS office when photographed on 17 February 1983, as Nos 08953 *Plymouth* and 08839 are seen shunting 'Speedlink' traffic, but such activity would soon decline. *John Smith, Terry Gough collection/ DHM*

PLYMOUTH FRIARY, the L&SWR's 'new' terminus, was nearer the city centre than North Road, but any such advantage was nullified by the detour necessary to reach it. Although the two stations were only about three-quarters of a mile apart 'as the crow flies', a Southern train had to travel nearly 3½ miles around the horseshoe route to reach it. Ivatt 2MT 2-6-2T No 41316 is arriving with 'gate set' No 373, forming the 12.50pm from Bere Alston on Monday 7 July 1958; the auto-trailers were so named because the centre exits were protected by metal gates rather than doors. Friary shed received the first of these 'Prairie' tanks in 1953, but from 1956 had a number of the type allocated to it, mostly replacing 'O2' and 'M7' 0-4-4Ts on local passenger and stock duties.

The freight yard was surrounded by housing and nearby residents mounted a legal challenge over shunting noise. This led to much of the work being transferred to Tavistock Junction Yard by May 1983, although a limited volume was handled here for a few more years. Now only a siding and run-round loop remain; the latter was retained mainly for the reversal of bitumen trains running to and from the Cattewater branch. A wide-angle lens view of the surviving track on 3 May 2012 includes the Radio Survey Train, but No 37604 has not quite managed to 'kiss' the buffers! *R. A. Lumber/DHM*

PLYMOUTH FRIARY passenger station opened on 1 July 1891, its unusual name deriving from having been built on the site of a medieval White Friars monastery that was dissolved by Henry VIII. Class 'T1' 0-4-4T No 17 is drawing (empty?) stock from the arrival platform on 8 July 1924; further stock is standing in the middle road, with the departure road empty. The main station building was on the up side, and can be glimpsed beyond the footbridge; the engine's exhaust is obscuring the up bay platform. Next to it is another bay road, known locally as the 'scenery road', as it was here that scenery was handled for touring theatre productions. The 45-lever 'B' signal box dated from the station's opening; the down bay is to its left. Out of view to the left are carriage sidings and the goods shed; the original engine shed was located further to the south until its closure in 1908. Branch trains to Turnchapel (and also Yealmpton between 1941 and 1947) normally used the bay platforms.

The 1980s view includes six cement wagons for Plymstock traffic and a rake of mineral wagons in the 'scenery' bay. The roads through the main platforms have been truncated; the warehouse on the left is on the site of the goods shed, and dates from about 1966 when it was used for National Carriers traffic. *Author's collection/C. M. Parsons*

PLYMOUTH FRIARY: The infrastructure remained largely intact after passenger services ceased on 15 September 1958, with the platforms busy handling goods and parcels traffic. The footbridge had, however, been removed by Good Friday 31 March 1961 when Class 'O2' 0-4-4T No 30183 was recorded on shunting duty at 5.00pm; the goods shed is now in view beyond the signal box. Passenger stock continued to be stabled here for a further couple of months.

The 'B' signal box closed in July the following year, the 'A' box was located near the junction with the Cattewater/Plymstock line, at the throat of the station layout and closed in April 1966. The station buildings were finally demolished during the spring of 1976, although the platforms survived for a few more years, as seen opposite. The 'new' warehouse was demolished to make way for a DIY store, constructed in 1990, and the rest of the terminus area was cleared in about 1992 for redevelopment. The flats are known as 'Friary Court'. *R. A. Lumber/DHM*

Sutton Harbour branch

NORTHEY'S SIDING: Due to silting problems at its tidal dock at Crabtree (near Marsh Mills), the Plymouth & Dartmoor Railway extended its route to Sutton Pool in December 1825, with a branch to Martin's (aka Laira) Wharf on the Cattewater. The South Devon Railway purchased the Sutton Harbour branch in 1851, converting it to mixed-gauge (broad and 4ft 6in) operation, though both gauges continued to use horse power at that time. When the SDR wanted to use locomotives to Sutton Harbour, it was impractical for these to share the track with horses, so the line was closed from 1856 to 1857 and rebuilt with a separate parallel track provided for each gauge. The 'Dartmoor'-gauge rails to Sutton Harbour survived until 1869. Northey's Siding, about a quarter of a mile from Friary Junction, was in use by 1901, and additional sidings were added in 1916, with a short-lived signal box, to serve a new munitions factory. The original siding was extended to connect with the Cattewater branch. Wolverhampton-built '2021' Class 0-6-0PT No 2038 is shunting on the loop near to the sidings at 12.10pm on 2 April 1952.

In about 1980 a relief road known as Gdynia Way was built over the route of the branch; in 2012 the Cattedown Road overbridge provides a link with the past. *Alan Lathey, Transport Treasury/DHM*

NORTH QUAY BRANCH JUNCTION was located just beyond the Cattedown Road bridge, the original branch continuing on to Lockyer's Quay and Bayly's Wharf on the south side of the harbour. The North Quay branch opened in 1879 and originally connected with the L&SWR's branch from Friary, the rails running as far as Sutton Wharf and Vauxhall Quay on the west side of the harbour. Near North Quay the rails crossed Sutton Road and a signal box was open from about 1914 to May 1956 to work the level crossing gates. The system beyond this crossing was closed by 1969. In a rare photo from the branch's later days, No D7573 (later 25223) is viewed from Cattedown Road as it heads down the truncated North Quay branch with a weed-killing train on 10 June 1973. The original route to the south side of the harbour is on the left; by then running only as far as the Commercial Road level crossing.

There was still some scrap traffic on the branch at that time, but not for much longer, as the line was closed at the end of 1973. The track was lifted by early 1975 and, as seen in March 2013, roads now follow both routes. *Bernard Mills/DHM*

BAYLY'S WHARF: The original branch served a goods depot and cement works adjacent to Commercial Road level crossing before running along the side of the harbour at Lockyer's Quay and Bayly's Wharf. For many years the Sutton Harbour system was serviced by two trains a day, with power usually provided by one of a number of veteran pannier tanks, their short wheelbase being suited to the sharp curvature of some sections of track on the quayside. The '1600' Class was designed to replace such locos and, although introduced in BR days, the class represents the last independent GWR design. Brand new 0-6-0PT No 1650 arrived at Laira at the end of 1954, and this engine provided the regular power on this duty until 1960 and its replacement by a Class 03 diesel shunter; it is seen shunting Bayly's Wharf in September 1959.

From June 1962 the branch only had one return service a day. The goods yard at Commercial Road was lifted in September 1969. With the demise of coal traffic off-loaded from coastal vessels at Bayly's Wharf, the section west of the crossing was also closed at the end of 1972. This part of the harbour is now home to Plymouth's fishing fleet. *Peter F. Bowles, R. Woodley collection/DHM*

Cattewater branch

NEAR LUCAS TERRACE HALT: While planning further railway development in the area, the Plymouth & Dartmoor Railway obtained powers to build a goods branch to the wharves on the Cattewater, on the northern bank of the River Plym. The line opened in August 1880 when it was worked by the L&SWR, which was allied to the P&DR in this enterprise; ownership of the line passed to the larger company just two years later. Just beyond Lucas Terrace Halt the line swung southwards on a sharp curve before being carried over two lattice girder bridges; the first 90-foot-long span crossed both the SDR's Sutton Harbour branch and the Lee Moor Tramway, the second, of 80 feet, passing over the Embankment Road. This section of the line as far as Cattewater Junction also carried trains running to Plymstock from 1892. The rails of the Sutton Harbour branch can be glimpsed in the foreground as Class 03 No D2128 returns west with the Plymstock goods on 28 April 1970.

The bridge span has been infilled since the Sutton Harbour track was recovered, and the route of the latter is now waste ground between here and Embankment Road. A cycleway/footpath has been built along the near side of the Cattewater branch, but was obscured by undergrowth in 2012. *John Medley/DHM*

CATTEWATER JUNCTION: This view from Laira (road) Bridge, looking north on Saturday 30 September 1961, includes the Cattewater branch (with crossing gates) in the foreground. In the shadows, bottom left, the Lee Moor Tramway can be glimpsed near its terminus at Martin's Wharf, which was located just beyond the other side of the road bridge. Meanwhile 'M7' 0-4-4T No 30034 is descending a short embankment, having just crossed Laira (railway) Bridge with the returning Plymouth Railway Circle's 'last train' from Turnchapel. The 24-lever junction signal box (open from 1898 to October 1963) can be seen in the middle distance, immediately to the left of the nearest telegraph pole. Until 1958 the twin tracks of Plymouth No 2 Curve to Mount Gould Junction had diverged here.

The 3 May 2012 Network Rail Radio Survey Train was the first train to traverse these rails in more than three years, No 37259 reaching the occupation crossing adjacent to the closed gates of the scrap loading point, the current extent of track on the truncated branch. (NB: The train is still moving, it terminated on the other side of the road bridge. A cycleway now occupies the embankment of the old Plymstock route. *Peter W. Gray/DHM*

NEAR CORPORATION WHARF: The Cattewater branch served many industrial locations in its short length, both the businesses and their associated sidings changing over the years. The Lee Moor Tramway crossed the branch beneath Laira road bridge before entering its terminus at Martin's Wharf. However, its conveyance of china clay to the quayside ended in about 1939. Nearby, the coal-fired Plymouth 'A' Power Station was built adjacent to Corporation Wharf in 1898 to supply electricity for the city's tram system. This closed in 1974, but a new power station had been opened in 1952 and this was also supplied with coal, although mainly by sea, for a while before being converted to oil-burning; it too has since closed with the site now occupied by a sewage treatment works. A scrap yard is also now located in this area and scrap metal was loaded on to EWS trains from April 2003 until about 2009; the traffic then ceased, reportedly due to the hauler being unable to meet the customer's needs. Further on, the branch once served the British Glues works, first established in 1914. 'B4' 0-4-0T No 84 (still to gain its BR number 30084) is shunting the works at 3.50pm on 7 March 1951.

The sidings to Corporation Wharf were removed in 1967, and the south end of the wharf can be noted on the right in October 2012. The branch trackbed is to the left of the foreground fence. *Alan Lathey, Transport Treasury/DHM*

MAXWELL ROAD LEVEL CROSSING: West of Corporation Wharf the branch diverged into two routes, the southern line hugging the waterside and serving Cattedown Wharves. Only the northern route had survived by 7 November 1995; No 08819 is crossing Maxwell Road, running light engine to the Conoco Depot where it will pick up empty bitumen tanks bound for Tavistock Junction Yard. The gates were manually operated by the travelling shunter. At that time, work was being undertaken on redeveloping the area's road system and a new road alignment runs to the left, where a crossing with automatic barriers was under construction. The loco will shortly pass through a 48-yard-long curving tunnel under Cattedown Road; clearance limitations through this tunnel and in some of the sidings restricted the types of locomotive used on the branch, and the 'B4' tanks dominated the work for many years. They were replaced by 204hp diesel-mechanical shunters (initially of Class 04, then '03'), before these gave way to Classes 08 and 09.

At the site of the crossing in October 2012, the road has been resurfaced but the trackbed was easily observed on each side. *Both DHM*

CATTEDOWN: 'B4' No 84 is shunting at 12.25pm on 9 January 1951; the two routes reunited here with the track in the foreground leading to Cattedown Wharves (behind the camera). A goods depot was provided west of the tunnel, while Esso Wharf is beyond the train. In 1888 the line was extended to Victoria Wharves; this final terminus was 2¼ miles from Friary.

In the 1960s the branch handled heavy fertiliser business, but latterly was mainly used for different oil-based traffics; it was gradually truncated and eventually terminated at the Conoco depot. The final traffic handled was bitumen from Fawley Refinery, but the last loads were received in April 2008, with the empties cleared on 16 May. Apparently the wagons were deemed to be life-expired, with no one prepared to invest in

their replacement; although quite possibly the tunnel would have precluded the use of longer modern designs. With 'no current or prospect of future traffic' Network Rail decided to further truncate the branch at the scrap loading point, and a contemporary report advised that most of the track beyond there had been lifted by February 2010. The gate in the 2012 photo marks the entrance to the former Conoco Depot. *Alan Lathey, Transport Treasury/ DHM*

Turnchapel branch

LAIRA BRIDGE: The L&SWR opened a branch from Cattewater Junction as far as Plymstock on 5 September 1892. To cross the River Plym, a lattice-type steel girder bridge was constructed parallel to a cast-iron bridge that had opened in 1827 to carry the main road from Plymouth to Kingsbridge. The railway bridge comprised six sections supported by tubular steel legs, both ends resting on limestone-faced abutments. The extension to Turnchapel opened in 1897, and a year later this bridge also carried GWR trains when that company's Yealmpton branch was opened. However, this was a freight-only route by 1 June 1953 when 'B4' No 30102 (now preserved) crossed the bridge with the returning Turnchapel goods at 4.00pm. The engine is fitted with a spark arrester, a prudent modification when working in the branch's timber yard!

The last freight traffic to be carried was cement from the Plymstock works, and LPG to a terminal adjacent to Plymstock station. The latter traffic had already ended by February 1987 when the cement trains also finished, with Blue Circle amending its manufacturing and distribution network. Citing over-capacity in the UK market, Plymstock was one of several works affected, with production reduced and the rail-served depots at Chacewater and Barnstaple closed. The rail bridge has survived, though, and now carries a gas main. *Alan Lathey, Transport Treasury/DHM*

PLYMSTOCK station was located in the 'V' of the junction between the Turnchapel and Yealmpton lines, with each branch having its own platform. The original station building was of an ornate corrugated construction; although an L&SWR facility, it was not provided with a canopy for its passengers, though there was one on the GWR side! A signal box stood on the south side of the line until 1935, when it was replaced by a new lever frame situated in the booking office. The station was badly damaged during the air raids of 1941 and the SR erected replacement 'temporary' buildings, which actually remained until demolition in the early 1960s. 'B4' No 30102 is seen again with the Turnchapel goods, but this time on Saturday 23 April 1955. The line to Yealmpton is in the foreground with the platform ramp just visible bottom left. Plymouth 'B' power station, adjacent to the Cattewater branch, can be seen in the distance beyond the bracket signal.

The cement plant was opened on a site to the north of the station in 1961 and, after the excavation and removal of much rock, a siding was laid into the works in 1963. Two years later work started on the construction of a depot to serve as an unloading point for liquefied petroleum gas. After all this traffic ended, the last train to Plymstock was the visit of the 'weed-killer' in April 1987! Track in the station area was lifted in 1994 and the cement works closed in 1998; the site remained undeveloped in 2012. *Peter F. Bowles, R.Woodley collection/DHM*

PLYMSTOCK: On 2 May 1959 the RCTS ran 'The Brunel Centenarian' railtour from Paddington to Saltash to celebrate the centenary of the opening of the Royal Albert Bridge; the seven coaches were hauled by 'Castle' No 7001 *Sir James Milne*. At Saltash the participants could join the 'Plymouth District Rail Tour' to Millbay and Plymstock, which featured 0-6-0PT No 6420 sandwiched between two pairs of auto-trailers (see page 62). At Plymstock the 'gricers' transferred to the sole-surviving ex-L&SWR 'gate set' No 373 headed by 'O2' No 30182, for a trip to Turnchapel. The 'push-and-pull' coaches had been specially worked down from Callington to operate this train. After returning to Plymstock, the ex-GWR auto-train was re-joined for a ride to Yealmpton, then it was back to North Road, from where the return to Paddington was appropriately powered by No 5069 *Isambard Kingdom Brunel*. From Plymstock station the Turnchapel branch curved southwards on a long embankment before crossing first the A379; the 'O2' can be seen crossing a second bridge over Pomphlett Road.

After closure the track here was lifted in early 1963, with demolition of the bridges in May of that year. The embankment was subsequently levelled, but a house on Pomphlett Road provides a link with the past in July 2012. Behind the camera the trackbed has been converted into a footpath and cycleway. *Peter F. Bowles, R. Woodley collection/DHM*

ORESTON: The branch south of Plymstock opened to passengers on 1 July 1897 with trains running from Friary, and this was the only intermediate station on this new section. Little more than a halt, it was a simple affair with one small building on a single 160-foot-long platform. A two-lever ground frame at the northern end of the station allowed access to a private siding that handled domestic coal traffic. The service provided by this branch was particularly susceptible to bus competition, and severe coal shortages led to a temporary closure to passengers from January to July 1951, effectively driving much of the remaining custom to road. The passenger service finally ceased from 10 September 1951, though goods trains continued to operate for a further ten years. With the scheduled closure of the branch to all traffic on Saturday 30 September 1961, the Plymouth Railway Circle organised a tour that day using Friary's 'M7' Class 0-4-4T No 30034, with eight brake-vans carrying nearly 90 'gricers'. The tour is seen here on its outward journey at the Oreston photo-stop. However, with a large amount of timber remaining to be cleared from Messrs Bayly's Yard, closure was postponed and the last goods train ran on 20 October.

The cycleway follows the route of the railway here; in 2012 another house (on the left) links these views.
Peter F. Bowles, R. Woodley collection/DHM

TURNCHAPEL: Just before reaching the station, the line crossed an inlet from the Cattewater into Hooe Lake by means of a manually operated swing bridge. This was interlocked with the signalling and controlled from a signal box next to the station; it was opened by the signalman, who would walk on to the bridge and hand-crank the mechanism, thus marooning himself until the bridge was closed again! 'O2' No 218 (later the Isle of Wight's No W33 *Bembridge*) is approaching with a train from Friary on 8 July 1924. Bayly's timber wharf is on the north side of the inlet; a siding from there runs beneath the bridge and climbs to join the branch in the distance. The branch ran on beyond the station to more wharves on the River Plym; these were taken over by the Admiralty during the First World War and provided further traffic for the line. The station and signal box were destroyed in November 1940 when nearby oil tanks were bombed, but goods trains were running again within a fortnight, and passenger services resumed soon after.

Prior to total closure the Admiralty traffic was negligible, and the only remaining business was the Oreston coal traffic and that from the timber yard, for which alternative facilities were provided. The station site was levelled after closure and enclosed within the confines of an oil storage depot; it was undergoing the early stages of redevelopment in July 2012. The bridge was dismantled in 1963, but the supports still remain. *H. C. Casserley/DHM*

Yealmpton branch

ELBURTON CROSS: A railway into the South Hams was promoted by the Plymouth & Dartmoor Railway, but the powers obtained by that company for the construction of a line from Plymstock to Yealmpton were subsequently transferred to the GWR. The branch opened on 17 January 1898 with four intermediate stations; Elburton Cross catered for the village after which it was named, but was the only station not providing any goods facilities. Trains ran from Millbay and initially passenger traffic grew steadily, but by the 1920s it was susceptible to bus competition. Until then all the intermediate stations had their own station masters, but these were replaced by senior porters working under the jurisdiction of Yealmpton's station master. Further attempts at cost-saving included the introduction of steam railmotors, but the decline continued, and passenger services ceased on 7 July 1930. Freight traffic was reasonably heavy, though, and a daily goods train continued to run. The 'past' photo shows the 'Plymouth District Rail Tour' of 2 May 1959 again, as No 6420 propels the tour past the derelict platform.

A road widening scheme here in 1977 involved the infilling of the cutting and removal of the bridge parapets, which were used as part of the infill. Since then a dwelling has been built on the station site, but the former 'kissing gate' station entrance survives to the left of the boundary wall. *Peter W. Gray/DHM*

YEALMPTON: The terminus was built as a through station, as it was originally planned that the branch would extend to Modbury, some 4 miles to the east. The track layout comprised a run-round loop, with a small goods yard, all controlled from a signal box. The latter closed when the passenger service ended in 1930 and 'one engine in steam' operation was employed. However, passengers were carried again from November 1941 following the Plymouth blitz, primarily to assist in the nocturnal evacuation of Plymouth's population to evade further bombing. With Millbay now closed, the new auto-worked service started at Friary, the regular engine being No 5412. Passenger numbers dropped once the war was over and the last passenger train ran on Saturday 4 October 1947. The 'Plymouth District' tour is seen arriving at the single platform on 2 May 1959.

Goods traffic continued until February 1960, latterly hauled by diesel shunters. The station has since been erased from the landscape with 'Riverside Walk' housing estate developed on its site. The approach road to this estate approximates the station approach, and a survivor in July 2012 is the brickwork (centre right) that once formed part of the eastern abutment of a bridge that carried the railway over the main road. *Peter W. Gray/DHM*

Towards Tavistock South

MARSH MILLS: The broad-gauge South Devon & Tavistock Railway opened on 22 June 1859, with all services provided by its parent company the South Devon Railway, running from its Millbay terminus. The actual branch ran for a distance of almost 13 miles from a junction with the SDR's main line to Tavistock. Marsh Mills station opened for goods traffic in 1860 and to passengers on 15 March of the following year. From 1834 to 1847 the Plympton branch of the Plymouth & Dartmoor Railway had crossed this site at right angles to the later branch. Viewed from the A38 overbridge, a '6400' Class 0-6-0PT waits to leave, propelling an auto-train from Tavistock South to Plymouth.

After most of the branch closed, this section was retained for goods trains, particularly china clay from a works just to the north. This traffic ended in May 2008 when the works closed, though overgrown track can be seen to the right of the Advance warning board in December 2012. The board applies to a level crossing installed just beyond the station in 1972 to give improved road access to the clay works. The cycleway in the left foreground runs over the former down platform. *Peter F. Bowles, R. Woodley collection/DHM*

MARSH MILLS: Another pannier tank, No 6430, is climbing the 1 in 60 gradient as it leaves with the 2.10pm Plymouth to Tavistock South train on 22 December 1962, the penultimate Saturday of passenger services over the branch. The 32-lever signal box can be glimpsed on the right; it was opened in March 1876 in time for the start of the L&SWR services from Lydford. It is thought that the branch, which is otherwise single-track, was doubled from here to the junction at this time. Additional levers were provided as trackwork expanded in the area. The siding to the china clay works opened in 1921 and is on the left of the train. From 1927 the clay was piped in slurry form from Lee Moor to the drying kilns here, and this no doubt helped to seal the eventual fate of the Lee Moor Tramway. The track in the foreground is a siding leading to the Coypool MOD Ordnance Depot, which opened in 1939.

The Coypool connection was officially closed on 31 March 1982, although it probably hadn't seen any use for several years. In the meantime the Plym Valley Railway Association had been formed and a depot established in the 'V' of the junction between the Tavistock and Coypool lines. This 31 March 2013 photo was taken from the railway's Marsh Mills platform, several hundred yards to the north of the original ones; as the new station could not be built on a grade, it was sited on raised and levelled ground. Saddle tank *Albert* is about to propel the 1300 departure to Plym Bridge. *Peter W. Gray/DHM*

LEE MOOR CROSSING: The Lee Moor Tramway was built to convey china clay from the Lee Moor area to Plymouth. It opened in 1854 but was poorly constructed, and had to be rebuilt, opening again in September 1858. The tramway shared the earlier Plymouth & Dartmoor Railway's 4ft 6in-gauge 'main line' from Plymouth to Crabtree, and from there it had exclusive use of the P&DR's Cann Quarry branch as far as Plym Bridge, the quarry having already closed. The promoters of the Tavistock branch had also originally intended to use the trackbed of the Cann Quarry branch south of Plym Bridge, but instead had to build a separate parallel alignment. The two lines crossed here, about halfway between Marsh Mills and Plym Bridge, and this meant that there were three different track gauges here during the period that the branch was 'mixed gauge'. A five-lever signal box was provided in 1895 to control the crossing, and is seen here in the early 1900s in a photo looking south towards Marsh Mills.

The box closed in 1955, but had been rarely manned for years, the tramway having largely closed down in 1945. The 'Drake's Trail' cycle route now follows the course of the tramway, but rails can be seen again, with Plym Valley Railway trains first running as far as here in 2001. The crossing-keeper is closing the gates behind the 1230 service from Plym Bridge on 31 March 2013. *Author's collection/DHM*

PLYM BRIDGE PLATFORM: A timber platform was opened here, about 1½ miles from Tavistock Junction, on 1 May 1906 to cater for trippers from Plymouth wishing to visit this beauty spot, which is surrounded by woodland. The unstaffed halt was rebuilt with a shorter concrete platform in 1949. 'Prairie' tank No 5544 is seen leaving with the 10.40am Saturdays-only Plymouth to Launceston train on 17 March 1962. The train is on an embankment, crossing the course of the P&D's Cann Quarry branch. The Lee Moor Tramway ran to the left after leaving that branch, and used the 1¼-mile-long Cann Wood Incline to climb 340 feet on an average gradient of 1 in 11.

The platform survived until 1970, when it was removed to be used as part of the new relocated St Ives station. The Plym Valley Railway has, however, erected a new platform, and trains started to run to here on 30 December 2012, thus marking the 50th anniversary of the line's closure. The original viewpoint is now

obscured by dense growth, so this view from behind the brake-van stop-block has Andrew Barclay 0-4-0ST No 2248 *Albert* 'tailing' the very first passenger train, a members' special, as it returns to Marsh Mills headed by Class 08 No 13002. The cycle trail can be seen on the left; it takes to the Tavistock branch formation here, thus precluding any future expansion of the railway. *Peter W. Gray/DHM*

CANN VIADUCT: The branch was extended to Launceston in July 1865 by the Launceston & South Devon Railway, another SDR subsidiary, giving a total length of about 32 miles. About three-quarters of a mile from Plym Bridge the line crossed the first of three timber viaducts that were constructed within a distance of about 1¼ miles; this one was built to carry the branch over the River Plym and the P&D's Cann Quarry branch (and an earlier canal). The viaduct was replaced by a six-arch 127-yard-long brick and stone structure in March 1907. On 17 March 1962 2-6-2T No 4566 has just passed over the viaduct with the 10.15am Launceston to Plymouth train; the derelict two-storey building on the right was originally home to several quarry workers' families.

The loco is currently preserved on the Severn Valley Railway. 'Drake's Trail' is a 21-mile cycle and walking route linking Plymouth and Tavistock. It is also part of the National Cycle Network and follows much of the branch formation, including the section from Plym Bridge to near the site of Clearbrook Halt. The now even more derelict building still survives on the right. *Peter W. Gray/DHM*

BICKLEIGH VIADUCT: The second of the three timber viaducts was Riverford, then followed Bickleigh Viaduct; both were rebuilt in 1893. Bickleigh Viaduct is 167 yards long and 123 feet high, comprises seven arches built of granite, and spans the valley of a tributary of the Plym. At 2.00pm on 17 March 1962 2-6-2T No 5544 is crossing with the 12.40pm Saturday's-only Launceston to Plymouth train. The original masonry piers of the timber viaduct can be seen to the left, with the Bickleigh fixed Down Distant signal just beyond the viaduct. A good view of Dartmoor's lower slopes can be obtained to the right. The ex-GWR 'Small Prairie' tank engines monopolised Launceston services for about 50 years; they often used the turntable at Launceston, thereby running chimney-first in both directions. During the branch's final years there were only three weekday passenger trains each way over its entire length, usually composed of two ex-GWR coaches; there were two additional Saturday workings, but no Sunday service.

Today the viaduct carries the trail, but is gradually being hidden by tree growth. This and the next four 'present' photos were taken on 6 September 2012. *Peter W. Gray/DHM*

BICKLEIGH: Just over half a mile north of the viaduct trains reached this station, which served a small village to the west. Opening with the branch, it became a crossing place in 1876 when extra capacity was needed to handle the L&SWR trains. A signal box was opened on the down platform, but this was subsequently replaced in 1913 by a 23-lever box located on the up platform. Its roof can be noted behind the second coach, as now preserved No 6430 waits while propelling its train from Tavistock to Plymouth on Saturday 18 August 1962. The platforms are widely spaced apart; a legacy of broad-gauge days. The auto-trains used on Plymouth suburban services were also used on this branch after the Second World War, but only on the five daily trains that terminated at Tavistock South. After the Saltash service was dieselised in 1960, four auto-trailers were retained for this branch. Use of this station increased in later years following the building nearby of Bickleigh Barracks, the base for a Royal Marines Commando battalion.

After closure most of the station area was cleared, although the edge of the down platform and the detached station master's house survive to the right, beyond the hedge. *Peter F. Bowles, R. Woodley collection/ DHM*

SHAUGH BRIDGE PLATFORM: The line continued over Ham Green Viaduct before reaching this halt, only just under a mile from Bickleigh. It was built beneath a road bridge on the site of an earlier siding used initially for loading low-grade iron ore, and subsequently china clay; the latter traffic was then handled at Bickleigh. The halt opened on 19 August 1907 and comprised a single curving platform with a corrugated-iron 'pagoda' shelter. Although it served the village of Shaugh Prior, a mile to the east, it was mainly intended for day-trippers from Plymouth who were attracted to the nearby woods and rivers, and to Dewerstone Rock, which rises to more than 600 feet on the southern edge of Dartmoor. There were tea rooms at the station until 1939. 'Prairie' tank No 4570 is approaching the platform from the south with an empty stock working at 12.10pm on 4 August 1962.

The second view shows the closed halt in 1969. Today, as seen in the third photograph, the cycle trail continues through here (the left 'leg' running at a higher level over the platform), and subsequently through the 308-yard-long Shaugh Tunnel. *Peter W. Gray/M. E. Hunt/DHM*

HORRABRIDGE: About 1½ miles beyond Yelverton, Horrabridge was one of the original stations and was always a crossing place. In earlier days it was one of the busier stations on the line, serving a wide area as well as the adjacent village. Initially it handled copper ore from local mines, and also dealt with a heavy coal and agricultural traffic. It served as a junction station for a short period as Yelverton station was not built when the Princetown branch first opened. A '4500' Class 2-6-2T is seen leaving with a train from Plymouth to Launceston on 18 August 1962; the signal box can be noted beyond the rear of the train on the up side, while the goods shed is to the left of the second coach.

'Drake's Trail' leaves the branch formation just before the site of Clearbrook Halt (now a dwelling) and only regains it at Horrabridge, where the station site has been developed for housing in recent years. The trail doubles as an access road, and the goods shed now forms part of a dwelling. After closure, the Yelverton station site reverted to its original owners and is now a densely wooded private nature reserve; permission could not be obtained for the cycleway to run through it. *Peter F. Bowles, R. Woodley Collection/DHM*

WALKHAM VIADUCT: About 1¼ miles north of Horrabridge the railway crossed the most notable structure on the line, a 367-yard-long, 132-foot-high viaduct, erected to span the valley of the River Walkham. Originally having a timber superstructure, it was rebuilt in 1910 when the existing masonry piers were raised with brickwork supporting 16 trussed girder spans. No 6438 propels a trailer forming the 8.45am Tavistock South to Plymouth train in August 1962.

The passenger service between Plymouth and Launceston ceased on Saturday 29 December 1962, coinciding with the start of the 'Great Freeze'. The penultimate trains in both directions became snowed up, and the last two scheduled services were unable to run. The viaduct was demolished in 1965, but in 2012 'Gem Bridge' was opened in the same location to carry 'Drake's Trail' over the valley. It cost £2.1 million and is 52 feet lower than its predecessor, so the formation on both approaches has been lowered accordingly. The trail beyond this point was further extended north through Grenofen Tunnel on 5 September 2012, the day before the 'present' photo was taken.

Tavistock South station and the line onwards to Launceston are covered in 'British Railways Past & Present' Nos 53 *North and West Devon* and 54 *East Cornwall*. *Peter F. Bowles, R. Woodley collection/DHM*

Princetown branch

DOUSLAND: The Plymouth & Dartmoor Railway was originally built to link Princetown with Plymouth, with a view to opening up Dartmoor for development. The line was opened from a dock on the River Plym at Crabtree to Foggintor Quarries in September 1823, and extended to Princetown by December 1826. It was never a great success and the only traffic of any consequence was granite from quarries at Foggintor, Ingra Tor and Swell Tor. The P&DR then came to an agreement to sell that part of its line from near Yelverton to Princetown to a subsidiary of the GWR. The standard-gauge Princetown Railway was built using much of the original route and opened on 11 August 1883. However, there was a delay in building the junction station at Yelverton due to opposition from local residents, and it did not open until May 1885. The village of Dousland was provided with the line's only original intermediate station, just over 1½ miles from Yelverton. On 31 December 1955 2-6-2T No 4568 is approaching a level crossing and its signal box as it leaves the station's single curving platform with the 1.22pm Saturdays-only train from Yelverton. The branch was worked by electric token in two sections, from Yelverton to Dousland, and Dousland to Princetown.

Since closure the site of the crossing has been obliterated, but the station building survives and has been converted into a bungalow. *Peter W. Gray/ DHM*

INGRA TOR HALT: Although the branch followed much of the Plymouth & Dartmoor Railway, there were deviations to alleviate some of the grades and curves on what was a highly circuitous route. The 'new' formation was about 10½ miles long, despite Yelverton and Princetown being only 6 miles apart 'as the crow flies'. The line gained more than 850 feet in height with a ruling gradient of 1 in 40, and trains travelled at a maximum speed of 20mph. The major deviation was to the east of Dousland, and it is on this section that Burrator & Sheepstor Halt was opened on 4 February 1924, one of three halts opened to encourage moorland visitors to travel by train on what was the only passenger line to ever penetrate into the heart of Dartmoor. The halt was located on an embankment high above the dam of a reservoir built in the 1890s to provide water for Plymouth. Another halt was opened on 2 March 1936 at Ingra Tor, about 6¼ miles from Yelverton and almost exactly 1,000 feet above sea level. Situated in a lonely spot with no road access and surrounded by magnificent scenery, the halt's timber platform and waiting shelter are recorded here in this 1955 view; a couple of isolated farmsteads can be seen in the valley below, and the quarry, by then disused, is just to the left. This halt is famous for the notice positioned in front of the shelter that advised passengers to keep their dogs on a lead 'in the interests of game preservation and for their protection against snakes etc.'

Sheep were a menace to engine crews, as they often wandered on to the track, and these rather than adders (or any 'etc'!) were the only creatures encountered in September 2012, although the hike across the bog proved to be rather soggy underfoot following a dismally wet summer. *Peter F. Bowles, R. Woodley collection/ DHM*

SWELL TOR: 'Prairie' tank No 4568 is descending the hillside with the 2.12pm train from Princetown on 31 December 1955; this was the regular engine for the last couple of months of the branch's existence. The train has not long passed a closed siding into Swelltor quarries, and is completing its navigation of a great loop encircling both King's Tor and Swell Tor. Visible immediately in front of the loco is a rough track that leads to the quarries on the hillside to the right, and then on to King Tor Halt. This was its timetable name, but the nameboard had 'King Tor Platform'. The halt was opened near Foggintor Quarries in April 1928 and is only about half a mile to the east of here, but 2 miles by train; it has been said that in good conditions an athletic person could get from Ingra Tor Halt to King Tor Halt faster than the train! The '4400' Class provided the regular power over the line from 1905 to 1955, but after the last of the class was withdrawn the '4500' type took over.

A 'permissive footpath' now follows the formation over the high moor, and the gate and fencing on the left survive in 2012 and help to identify the location. *Peter W. Gray/DHM*

PRINCETOWN: The famous prison was built in 1806 to house captives of the Napoleonic Wars, on land provided by the Prince of Wales from his Duchy of Cornwall estate (hence the name). The town grew up near the prison, but suffered greatly when the latter closed in 1816. However, the arrival of the Plymouth & Dartmoor line helped the employment position with work in the quarries. The prison was reopened in 1850 as a gaol for convicted criminals, particularly those serving long sentences, and subsequently provided business for the 'new' railway when it opened. The branch was the highest in England, with its terminus 1,373 feet above sea level. Viewed from an occupation bridge, the single platform can be seen beyond the 14-lever signal box in August 1955, with the goods shed centre right and the small engine shed far right. The P&D's terminus had been a little further to the east.

The quarries closed in the 1920s and the branch always struggled for its existence in a sparsely populated area, although tourists could throng to the trains on fine days at holiday times. There has to be some doubt whether it ever paid its way, and it was claimed when closure was proposed that for every £1 in revenue, £7 was being spent on operating costs! Although the validity of such statistics has often been questioned when a line's future was being considered, there is every chance that they were accurate here. The last trains ran on Saturday 3 March 1956, and track-lifting started here in the following October. The former railway houses on the left provide a link with the past in 2012. *R. A. Lumber/DHM*

Tavistock Junction to Totnes

TAVISTOCK JUNCTION: After running alongside the Plym Estuary for more than half a mile from Laira Junction, Old Oak Common's 'King' Class 4-6-0 No 6025 *King Henry III* crosses the river near Crabtree with the 4.10pm Plymouth to Paddington train on 18 February 1962; Tavistock Junction is immediately behind the camera. All of the 'Kings' were withdrawn from service that year, with No 6025 one of the last four to go in December.

The photo was taken from a bridge carrying the driveway to Saltram House, formerly the family seat of the Earl of Morley. The house had been sold to the National Trust in 1957, but the bridge was still known locally as 'Lord Morley's Bridge', and has since been superseded by the A38 dual-carriageway. A footbridge has been erected on the west side of the flyover and the view from this on 16 October 2012 includes the 0741 Penzance to Paddington HST crossing the Plym. The 'sails' in the right background are part of a tensioned fabric roof constructed above a superstore built in the early 1990s. *Terry Nicholls/DHM*

TAVISTOCK JUNCTION: Turning in the opposite direction from the previous photos, we see 'Manor' Class 4-6-0 No 7815 *Fritwell Manor* piloting a down train in the 1950s. The branch to Tavistock and Launceston curves to the left; it was double-track for about a quarter of a mile as far as Marsh Mills station. In the left foreground part of the original 1876 signal box can be seen; this opened in connection with the conversion of the track between Lydford and Plymouth to mixed gauge, and was replaced by a new box in 1916 when a marshalling yard was opened. The yard comprised up and down goods loops, with four sidings on the up side of the line and eight on the down side. The second box was constructed about 11 chains to the east and can be seen centre right. It contained a 56-lever frame, but when the yard was enlarged in 1941 the box was extended and a new frame of 105 levers installed.

There was no direct connection to Marsh Mills from the yard, so any trains between those points had to reverse on the main line. After the closure of the Launceston branch, the curve to Marsh Mills was diverted in 1965 to join the end of one of the sidings in the up yard; nine other sidings had to be shortened to accommodate this new single-line chord. The signal box closed on 10 November 1973 when control passed to the Plymouth panel. The 'present' photo was taken from the A38 slip road, a little to the east of the 'past' view; the 1252 Exeter St David's to Plymouth service (No 150219) is approaching on 21 July 2012.

Peter F. Bowles, R. Woodley collection/DHM

TAVISTOCK JUNCTION YARD: Viewed from Cot Hill Bridge, No D1011 *Western Thunderer* is heading away from the camera on 9 December 1970, running light engine over the down main line. To its left are the down goods loop and down reception line. With the advent of the Second World War and the need for extra siding accommodation in the Plymouth area, the down yard was extended from eight to 19 sidings in 1940-41. At the same time the up side was extended from four to 18 sidings. A final extension to the yard came in 1958 when it was planned to close Laira Yard to make way for the new diesel depot and carriage sidings, and seven sidings were added to the up side. Overall the yard's capacity was increased by 373 to a total accommodation of 1,905 wagons. Modernised lighting was installed and a new administration block was built on the up side; this can be noted above the leading cab of the 'Western'.

This expansion proved to be something of a false dawn, however, with contraction commencing in the 1960s. Over the years the entire down yard has been removed apart from one siding. Currently the yard sees little use; it does, however, handle steam-powered railtours that terminate at Plymouth. On 28 July 2012 4-6-2s Nos 60163 *Tornado* and 71000 *Duke of Gloucester* sandwich their support coach as they reverse into the yard, where they will be serviced; they have just been turned via the 'Laira triangle'. *Bernard Mills/DHM*

TAVISTOCK JUNCTION YARD: Looking east towards Plympton from the same bridge, maroon-liveried Class 52 No D1009 *Western Invader* is approaching with the 1430 Paddington to Penzance train in 1969. Access to the down goods loop (on the right) from the east had been removed in 1966, but the track is still in place as a siding. The up goods loop had been taken out of use in 1967; the trackbed is to the left of the main running lines. Beyond this are a headshunt and the up departure line.

The marshalling yard closed on 4 January 1971, the work transferring to Friary. This left a modicum of local and engineer's traffic here, but about ten years later there was an increase in activity and, after some upgrading work, the handling of most 'Speedlink' traffic was transferred from Friary in 1983. The up yard has been reduced in size, and has about half the number of sidings that were available at its maximum. Traffic has reduced substantially over the years, as various flows have been lost; currently the only regular freight train to call is a weekly service carrying gas oil for Laira and Penzance depots. Although other traffic passes through Plymouth, the only freight business to currently emanate from the city are the very occasional military and nuclear trains, a sad story for a city of its size. Another 28 July 2012 view has *Duke of Gloucester* in the headshunt after arriving from Plymouth station with the empty stock from the 'Tamar Devonian' railtour. *Bernard Mills/DHM*

PLYMPTON station opened on 15 June 1848, just over a month after the South Devon Railway commenced operations to Laira Green. It was located at the foot of Hemerdon Bank and served an ancient stannary town that has more than 1,100 years of recorded history. However, the station was an early casualty, and closed to passengers on 2 March 1959. Exactly two months later 4-6-0 No 7820 *Dinmore Manor* approaches with an up six-coach train; this class was limited to a load of 252 tons for an unassisted climb of the bank. The start of an up refuge siding can be seen next to the engine. The small goods yard is on the left; this occupied the site of the terminus of a Plymouth & Dartmoor Railway branch that was closed to allow for the construction of the SDR. The signal box was located on the down platform.

The up refuge siding was taken out of use in 1962, the goods yard closed in June 1964 and, with the closure of the signal box in June 1967, Plympton lost its final connection with the railway. 'Voyager' No 221124 is working the 0828 Penzance to Glasgow service on 16 October 2012; housing has been built on the goods yard. *Peter F. Bowles, R. Woodley collection/DHM*

HEMERDON BANK comprises a 2-mile climb eastwards from Plympton, with a short section on a gradient of 1 in 41, though mostly at a constant 1 in 42. This is one of the three major banks on the SDR route from Newton Abbot, an unfortunate legacy of the 'atmospheric caper'. Although much of the line was originally single-track, the section from Hemerdon 'summit' to Laira Green was double from its opening. Part of the bank passed through woodland, and in the autumn trains could slip to a standstill due to leaves falling on the line (this is not the recent phenomenon that some would suggest!). In about 1946 a telephone was installed at the point where the line entered the woods, and if a train was stranded the guard was then able to inform the Plympton signalman. 'West Country' 4-6-2 No 34024 *Tamar Valley* is storming up the bank with an 'exchange duty', the 2.30pm Plymouth to Newton Abbot local train, on 5 July 1958. With the closure of five stations between Plymouth and Brent in 1959, and the subsequent reduction in services, the SR 'Pacifics' lost their jobs on the interchange workings over the WR between Plymouth and Exeter.

The 0835 Penzance to Paddington HST (power cars Nos 43196 and 43009) nears the top of the bank on 30 December 2012. *Peter W. Gray/DHM*

HEMERDON SIDING: A signal box was opened at the top of the bank in 1893 when the line was doubled from Cornwood, but was replaced in 1907 when the up and down sidings were converted to goods loops; these could hold 58 and 60 wagons respectively in addition to an engine and brake-van, and were adapted for use by passenger trains in 1930. The 'new' box was of timber construction and located on the up side; at the insistence of a local landowner the rear was painted green so that it would blend in with the surrounding countryside! This box was declared unsafe after the woodwork had been attacked by insects, and a new brick-built structure with a 35-lever frame was opened on the down side in 1930. This can be seen on the left as No 6931 *Aldborough Hall* pilots a 'Castle' Class engine on an up train, probably in the late 1950s; in the distance a goods train is leaving the down loop.

The signal box was closed on 17 December 1973, and the down loop was removed after being severely damaged by a freight train derailment. The up loop is still used, though, and Nos 37667 *Meldon Quarry Centenary* and 37668 are leaving it with the 1655 Fridays-only St Blazey to Bescot china clay train on 3 September 1999; this was the last diagrammed working for the class on this train, with Classes 60 or 66 taking over the following week. *Author's collection/DHM*

BLACHFORD VIADUCT: Just over 1½ miles from Hemerdon, a station served the village of Cornwood from 1852 until 1959; it was situated in the half-mile between Slade and Blachford Viaducts. These are two of five such structures in a 7-mile stretch that carry the railway across valleys cut out by streams flowing down from Dartmoor. All were originally built of timber on granite piers but were replaced with new structures in 1893-94 under the supervision of engineer Sir James Inglis. The curving 309-yard-long Blachford Viaduct has rock-faced granite piers supporting ten arches of blue engineering brick, with brick parapets. 'Castle' Class No 5069 *Isambard Kingdom Brunel* has just crossed the Yealm Valley with the returning RCTS 'Brunel Centenarian' railtour on 2 May 1959 (see page 88).

Standing 'inside the fence' is not permitted these days, not that much can be seen from the overgrown trackside! The 1532 Plymouth to Newton Abbot service (No 150261) is seen from an occupation bridge on 28 July 2012. A Network Rail radio tower now stands beyond the west end of the viaduct. *Peter W. Gray/DHM*

IVYBRIDGE was originally a small village that grew following the opening of a large paper mill beside the fast-flowing waters of the River Erme. Its station was built high on the hillside with a panoramic view of the town, and opened on 15 June 1848, six weeks after the SDR started running to Plymouth. The railway crosses the Erme immediately east of the station, and when the viaduct was rebuilt in 1894 the new track alignment required the construction of a new down platform. The up platform was widened to 'meet' the new formation, and the main chalet-style building is on the right as 4-6-0s Nos 7820 *Dinmore Manor* and 6013 *King Henry VIII* pass at 4.40pm with the 1.10pm Penzance to Paddington train.

The station closed to passengers on 2 March 1959 and was largely demolished in 1964. Goods traffic ended in 1965, though the yard was then used for loading china clay for a period from 1968. Access for a similar view today is impossible, but this 16 October 2012 scene from near the site of the cattle dock (to the west of the station) includes the goods shed, which is now occupied by a motor trader. 'Voyager' No 220033 forms the 1625 Plymouth to Leeds service. The town's population has grown dramatically from the 1960s and it is now very much a dormitory for Plymouth; in July 1994 a new station was opened more than half a mile to the east to cater for this expanding population. *Peter W. Gray/DHM*

WRANGATON is a small hamlet on the southern edge of Dartmoor, but was provided with the only intermediate station when the SDR first opened from Totnes. Situated adjacent to a crossroads, it acted as a railhead for a wide area, including the town of Kingsbridge, which was served by stage coaches. Indeed, the station was soon renamed Kingsbridge Road following a petition from the inhabitants of that town, but reverted to its original name in 1895 after the branch to Kingsbridge had opened. The high-level station building can be seen on the left as 'Modified Hall' No 7916 *Mobberley Hall* and 'Mogul' No 6334 pass with an up perishables train at 5.15pm on 7 April 1958. They are near the summit of the route as they approach a short 69-yard-long tunnel that takes the railway beneath the crossroads. The goods yard is at the west end of the station, with additional sidings serving the Admiralty's Monksmoor Depot opposite on the north side of the line.

The station closed to passengers on 2 March 1959 and to goods on 9 September 1963. The station building survives as a dwelling, but is obscured on 16 October 2012 as the 1723 Plymouth to Leeds Cross Country service sweeps by. *Peter W. Gray/DHM*

BRENT station was always known by this name despite being built on the northern edge of South Brent, a small town that takes its name from Brent Hill, a little further to the north. It is suggested that the town experiences a higher rainfall than its neighbours, no doubt due to its proximity to Dartmoor. During the 'Great Blizzard' of March 1891, heavy snow fell continuously for two days and the 'Zulu' (the 3.00pm from Paddington) became stranded in Brent; most of the 40 passengers had to either remain on the train or use the waiting room, there being little accommodation in the town. The train was more than three days late when it finally reached Plymouth. Road bridges cross the railway at each end of the station, that at the west end providing the vantage point as 'Castle' Class No 5085 *Evesham Abbey* steams through with the 'Cornishman', the 9.00am from Wolverhampton to Penzance, at 3.00pm on 26 March 1960; it will shortly cross a bridge over the River Avon.

The 1157 Paddington to Penzance HST (power cars Nos 43150 and 43022) speeds by on 18 November 2012. *Peter W. Gray/DHM*

BRENT station opened on 15 June 1848, about six weeks after the SDR commenced services. The broad-gauge line was single-track through here, and the original platform and station building were on the down side. A crossing loop was provided in 1875 and the line was doubled in 1893, with the section from Rattery opening in May, and that part west to Wrangaton in October. The station was rebuilt at that time to accommodate both the doubling and the opening of the Kingsbridge branch. Access was now gained via the up side, where the main buildings were located. A 550-foot-long island platform was provided to serve down trains, with branch trains running from its outer face, adjacent to the goods yard. A 66-lever signal box was opened on the down platform in October 1893, in time for the branch's opening two months later, and this can be seen in this view looking west as an up train arrives, probably in the first decade of the 20th century; the substantial goods shed is on the left.

The signal box closed in December 1973, but was subsequently used as a cabin by permanent way staff. It is passed by power car No 43156 heading 'The Cornish Riviera', the 0844 Penzance to Paddington service, on 23 May 2012. The goods shed also survives and is now occupied by the 'Primrose Junction Dental Centre'. *Author's collection/DHM*

BRENT: Looking in the opposite direction from the previous views, 2-6-2T No 4582 nears its destination with the 4.15pm train from Kingsbridge on 27 August 1953. The main line to Totnes is curving on a descending grade to the left; in just over a mile, and near the top of Rattery bank, it will pass through the only other tunnel between Plymouth and Totnes, the 867-yard-long twin-bore Marley Tunnel. This was not needed in engineering terms, but dug solely to appease the landowner who refused to have the railway running over his estate.

Brent station lost much of its raison d'être when the branch closed in September 1963. Its location on the northern edge of the town meant that most residents had easier access to buses on the main road to the south, and the station closed on 5 October 1964. On 18 November 2012 the 1256 Penzance to Paddington HST passes the site of the junction. *Derek Frost/DHM*

TOTNES nestles in the hollow of the Dart Valley, and straight from the platform westbound trains start to climb another of the notorious 'South Devon banks'. By the time it has reached Rattery, a train will have climbed 351 feet in just over 4½ miles from Totnes. The working timetable gave the ruling gradient as 1 in 54, although it is 1 in 46 at its steepest and the lower part of the climb is also beset by severe reverse curves. The grades ease after Tigley, but the uphill climb continues all the way to Wrangaton, a total distance of about 9 miles. In steam days there were normally two banking engines on duty at Totnes to assist freight trains on the severe banks on either side of the station, Rattery to the west and Dainton to the east. The latter is in prospect for two 4-6-0s, No 4976 *Warfield Hall* and an unidentified 'Castle', as they drop down into Totnes with an up train in July 1960. Drivers were instructed not to make up lost time by over-zealous downhill running on the banks, and a limit of 50mph applied on the descent from Wrangaton. By this time North British Type 2 diesel-hydraulics were beginning to perform much of the assistance work over the banks.

'Voyager' No 221130 eases down the bank forming the 1125 Plymouth to Dundee service on 15 September 2012. *Rail Photoprints Collection/DHM*

TOTNES: Looking in the opposite direction from the bypass road bridge on the same day, 'Modified Hall' No 7906 *Fron Hall* is piloting 'Warship' No D815 *Druid* as they tackle the initial 1 in 66 grade with a down express. They have passed non-stop through the station, which is just beyond the distant road overbridge. The sidings centre right are on the site of an engine shed that was built in 1847 to house banking engines and had been demolished by 1904; a locomotive turntable was also located here and was in use until about 1909. 'Warships' were allowed to haul 400 tons unassisted on passenger workings over the South Devon banks, an increase over steam loadings; a solo 'King', for example, was permitted 360 tons if the standard point-to-point timing was to be maintained.

The only trains that would require assistance over the banks today are certain heavy freight workings, but current practice is for these to be split into two portions for this part of their journey. The 0906 Paddington to Plymouth HST (power cars Nos 43042 and 43141) attacks the bank on 15 September 2012. *Rail Photoprints Collection/DHM*

TOTNES is an ancient town with a recorded history dating back to AD 907, when a defensive fort was built. It became an important market town due to both its location on one of the main roads through Devon and the easy navigation of the River Dart. The SDR opened from Newton Abbot to Totnes on 20 July 1847 with its station sited a little over half a mile from the town centre; originally single-track, the line had been doubled as far as Totnes by 1857. Signalling methods were still somewhat primitive at that time, but an installation of fully locking points and signals was made here in 1873. A signal box was provided on the down platform from 1894 to 1923, when it was replaced by a new 111-lever box located at the east end of the up platform. This became a 'fringe box' to the Plymouth panel on 17 December 1973. 'Peak' No 46021 is entering the up platform road on 18 August 1979 with the 1402 Newquay to Birmingham summer Saturdays train; the platform loops had been extended in 1930.

The semaphores disappeared when the box closed on 9 November 1987, and the station's signalling is now controlled from the Exeter panel. 'Voyager' No 220033 is arriving forming the 0940 Penzance to Manchester service on 28 September 2012. *Both DHM*

TOTNES: Locomotives were used when the SDR started running to here, but at that time it was still the intention to use the 'atmospheric' system through to Plymouth. Pipes were laid over most of the route to Totnes, and a building housing the pumping engines was completed adjacent to the station. However, the concept was abandoned in September 1848 and no trains actually used this method beyond Newton Abbot; the engine house was later used for a period as a cider factory. At 2.59pm on Sunday 6 September 1953 Nos 6822 *Manton Grange* and 6023 *King Edward II* speed over the down through line with the 10.30am Paddington to Penzance train. The pilot loco's exhaust is partially obscuring a tall chimney bearing the legend 'Daws Creameries'; from 1934 the company occupied the engine house as a milk factory. It was purchased by Cow & Gate Ltd in 1936 and provided a good deal of business for the railway – glass-lined milk tanks can be noted to the left of the 'Grange'.

Milk traffic was lost to the railway in 1980 and the creamery closed in 2007; a subsequent attempt to demolish the engine house was thwarted, and the building has been listed by English Heritage. Power cars Nos 43005 and 43159 pause with the 1000 Penzance to Paddington 'Cornishman' on 28 September 2012. *Derek Frost/DHM*

Kingsbridge branch

AVONWICK was one of three intermediate stations when the GWR opened the branch on 19 December 1893. About 2½ miles from the junction at Brent, the station was actually located in the small community of Beneknowle, about half a mile south of the village that it purported to serve. It became an unstaffed halt after nationalisation, and 'small Prairie' No 4561 is seen leaving the single platform with the 10.10am Brent to Kingsbridge train on 1 August 1960. Much of the branch follows the valley of the River Avon, which flows beyond the trees on the left.

The GWR introduced camping coaches in 1934, and all of the intermediate stations were selected as sites for these, an indication of the area's beauty. At Avonwick the coaches were kept on a loop siding to the north of the platform, but this activity ended in the 1950s when the siding was removed.

Although its canopy has been removed, the stone station building survives as a dwelling. All the 'present' photos on this branch were taken on 24 July 2012.
Peter W. Gray/DHM

GARA BRIDGE: Three miles further south, the predominantly rural nature of the line is exemplified by this view of the branch's only crossing station, which was provided with a long passing loop. The ex-GWR 2-6-2Ts worked the line's services for much of its existence, and for the last couple of years of steam operation Newton Abbot shed maintained Nos 4561, 5558 and 5573 for use on the branch. The former is seen again on 8 June 1961 as it leaves with the 2.30pm train from Brent. The loco has just crossed the Avon, one of ten such crossings on the 12½-mile line. The branch handled considerable parcels traffic and most trains included at least one parcels van. Camping coaches can be observed in the siding just behind the van; two were brought to both Gara Bridge and Loddiswell (the other intermediate station) for the last time for the 1961 season. The 24-lever signal box is at the end of the up platform, and controlled an adjacent level crossing; the hamlet is to the right.

Since closure the station building has been converted into a private house. No 4561 has been preserved, and is based on the West Somerset Railway. *Peter W. Gray/DHM*

KINGSBRIDGE: 'Prairie' tank No 5558 is awaiting departure from the curved main platform of the terminus with the 11.00am train to Brent on 5 August 1960. A bay platform is to the right, from which a spur runs to the single-road loco shed, just beyond the water tower. A short carriage shed is also visible immediately to the left of the loco. The sizeable goods yard is also to the left, with the large goods shed behind the camera.

The branch service was dieselised with single-car units from the start of the summer timetable on 12 June 1961, although steam continued to help out with the augmented Saturday service that summer. Goods trains were also steam-powered for a while longer before being handled by North British Type 2 diesel-hydraulics. The last trains ran on 14 September 1963, and track-lifting began just two months later. The site of the station is now the 'Station Yard Industrial Estate'. The 'present' scene is looking in the opposite direction, the 'past' viewpoint being within the large building seen in the background.

The station building survived in commercial use for many years, but was demolished in 2009; the goods shed was, however, still standing in 2012. *Hugh Ballantyne, Rail Photoprints/ DHM (2)*

INDEX OF LOCATIONS

BIBLIOGRAPHY

Binding, John *Brunel's Cornish Viaducts* (Pendragon, 1993)
Burkhalter, Paul *Devonport Dockyard Railway* (Twelveheads Press, 1996)
Cooke, R. A. *Atlas of the GWR* (Wild Swan, 1988)
   Track Layout Diagrams of the GWR, Sections 12 & 14 (R. A. Cooke, 1976)
Crosier, Larry *Mechanical Signalling in Plymouth* (Signalling Record Society, 2000)
Gibson, Bryan *The Lee Moor Tramway* (Plymouth Railway Circle, 1993)
Gough, Terry *The Tamar and Tavy Valleys* (Past & Present Publishing, 2001)
Gray, Peter W. *Rail Trails: South West* (Silver Link Publishing, 1992)
Gregory, R. H. *The South Devon Railway* (Oakwood Press, 1982)
Horton, Philip *The Beeching Legacy: The West Country* (Silver Link Publishing, 2010)
Kingdom, Anthony R. *The Plymouth, Tavistock & Launceston Railway* (ARK Publications, 1990)
   The Yelverton to Princetown Railway (Forest Publishing, 1991)
   The Plymouth to Turnchapel Railway (ARK Publications, 1996)
   The Plymouth to Yealmpton Railway (ARK Publications, 1998)
Leitch, Russell *Plymouth's Railways in the 1930s* (RCTS, 2002)
Mills, Bernard *Steam around Plymouth* (Tempus, 2003)
   The Branch (Plymouth-Tavistock South-Launceston) (Plym Valley Railway, 1983)
Mitchell, David *'British Railways Past & Present' No 8 Devon* (Past & Present Publishing, 1991)
   No 17 Cornwall (Past & Present Publishing, 1993)
   No 53 North and West Devon (Past & Present Publishing, 2006)
   No 54 East Cornwall (Past & Present Publishing, 2006)
Mitchell, Vic and Smith, Keith *Newton Abbot to Plymouth* (Middleton Press, 2001)
   Plymouth to St Austell (Middleton Press, 2001)
   Tavistock to Plymouth (Middleton Press, 1996)
   Branch Lines around Plymouth (Middleton Press, 1997)
   Branch Lines to Launceston and Princetown (Middleton Press, 1998)
Nicholas, John and Reeve, George *The Okehampton Line* (Irwell Press, 2001)
Smith, Martin *An Illustrated History of Plymouth's Railways* (Irwell Press, 1995)
Williams, Ken and Reynolds, Dermot *The Kingsbridge Branch* (OPC, 1977)